HOW COMPUTER PROGRAMMING WORKS

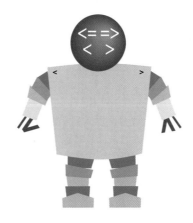

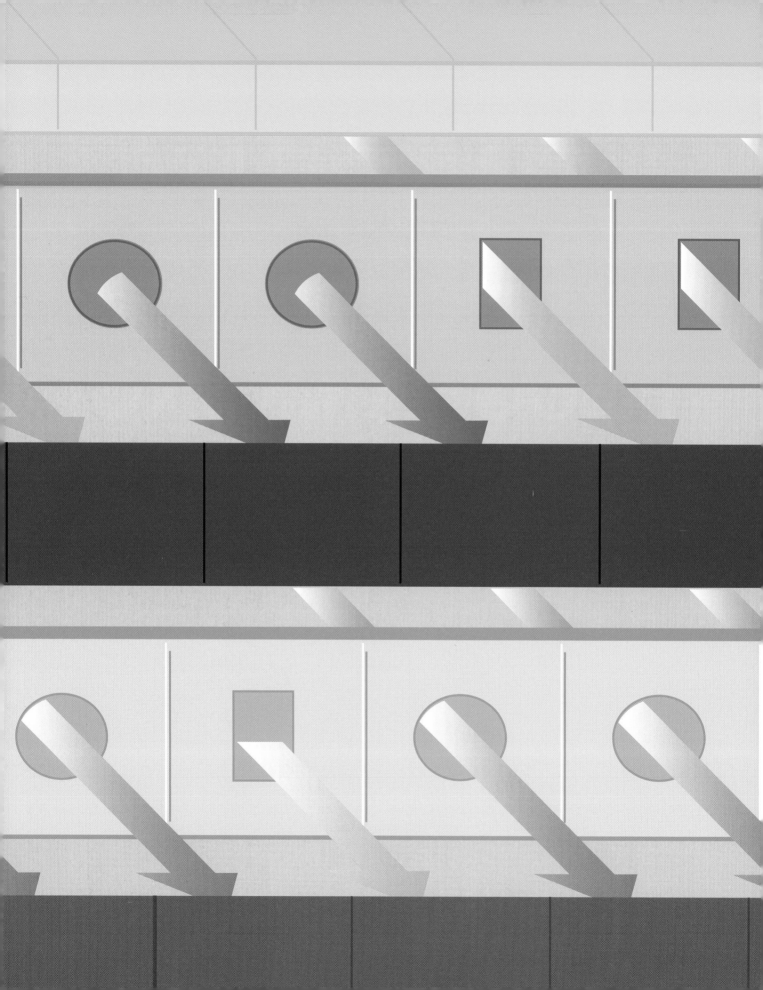

HOW
COMPUTER
PROGRAMMING
WORKS

DANIEL APPLEMAN

Illustrated by
SARAH ISHIDA

apress™

First printing by Ziff-Davis, 1994.
Copyright ©2000 by Daniel Appleman

Library of Congress Cataloging-in-Publication Data

Appleman, Daniel.
  How computer programming works / Daniel Appleman ; illustrated by Sarah Ishida.
    p.   cm.
  Includes bibliographical references and index.
  ISBN 1-893115-23-2 (softcover : alk. paper)
    1. Computer programming.   I. Title

QA76.6 A654 2000
005.1—dc21   00-025265

ISBN (pbk): 1-893115-23-2
Printed and bound in the United States of America
1 2 3 4 5 6 7 8 9 10

Distributed to the book trade worldwide by Springer-Verlag New York, Inc.
175 Fifth Avenue, New York, NY 10010
In the United States, phone 1-800-SPRINGER; orders@springer-ny.com
www.springer-ny.com

For information on translations, please contact APress directly:
Apress, 901 Grayson Street, Berkeley, CA 94710-2617
www.apress.com

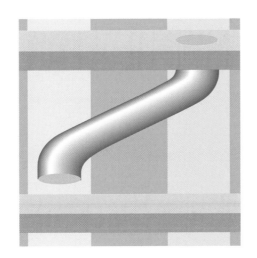

Introduction.............................xi

PART 1

Getting Started

1

Chapter 1
What Are Hardware and
Software?.................................4

Chapter 2
What Is a Computer
Language?...............................10

PART 2

Data

17

Chapter 3
Variables................................20

Chapter 4
Numeric Values.....................26

Chapter 5
Text Variables 30

Chapter 6
Boolean and Flag
Variables................................36

Chapter 7
Pointers 44

PART 3

Code

49

Chapter 8
Statements and Operators.......52

Chapter 9
Blocks and Functions 58

Chapter 10
Program Flow 62

Chapter 11
Variable Declaration and
Scoping 66

PART 4

Organizing Data

73

Chapter 12
Arrays 76

Chapter 13
Structures 82

Chapter 14
Stacks and Queues.................88

Chapter 15
Linked Lists............................**94**

Chapter 16
Decision Trees **100**

Chapter 22
Simulations **140**

Chapter 27
How the C Language
Works...................................**178**

Chapter 28
How BASIC Works..............**182**

Chapter 29
How Event-Driven Program-
ming Works **188**

Chapter 30
How User Interface Design
Works...................................**192**

Chapter 31
How Object-Oriented,
Component, and Client-Server
Programming Works.............**198**

Chapter 32
How Internet Programming
Works...................................**206**

Chapter 33
How Embedded Programming
Works, and How to Program
Your VCR.............................**210**

Where Do You Go
from Here?...........................**214**

Index **216**

PART 5
Algorithms
105

Chapter 17
Searching and Scanning **108**

Chapter 18
Recursion **114**

Chapter 19
Sorting..................................**120**

Chapter 20
Working with Files...............**126**

Chapter 21
Graphics **132**

PART 6
Methods and Tools
145

Chapter 23
How Computer Languages
Work **148**

Chapter 24
Why Are There So Many
Computer Languages? **152**

Chapter 25
How Programmers Work......**158**

PART 7
Languages and
Technologies
169

Chapter 26
How Assembly Language
Works...................................**172**

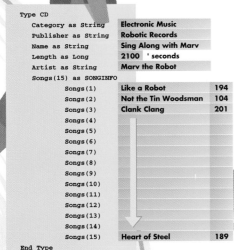

```
Type CD
    Category as String      Electronic Music
    Publisher as String     Robotic Records
    Name as String          Sing Along with Marv
    Length as Long          2100  ' seconds
    Artist as String        Marv the Robot
    Songs(15) as SONGINFO
        Songs(1)     Like a Robot        194
        Songs(2)     Not the Tin Woodsman 104
        Songs(3)     Clank Clang          201
        Songs(4)
        Songs(5)
        Songs(6)
        Songs(7)
        Songs(8)
        Songs(9)
        Songs(10)
        Songs(11)
        Songs(12)
        Songs(13)
        Songs(14)
        Songs(15)    Heart of Steel       189
End Type
```

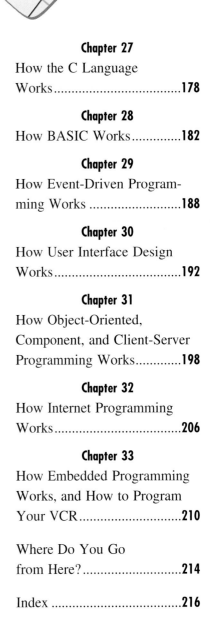

Every book is a collaboration, and I had a great deal of help in bringing this book to life. First and foremost, I would like to thank Sarah Ishida for her remarkable illustrations. She was able to creatively interpret even the clumsiest sketches. I deeply appreciate the efforts of Miriam Liskin, who went far beyond the call of duty as technical editor, not only ensuring the accuracy of the contents, but providing valuable suggestions on content and presentation as well. Thanks also to Virginia Howland for sharing her perspective on user interface design for Chapter 30.

Many thanks to MaryAnn Brickner, Henry Krell and Rhea Talbert at Springer, and the compositors at Matrix, who did a wonderful job resurrecting this new edition and incorporating the many changes and new graphics.

And thanks again to the original group from Ziff-Davis Press (which no longer exists) who worked on the first edition—wherever they may be now: Valerie Haynes Perry, Janna Hecker Clark, Carol Henry, Kim Haglund, Ami Knox and Cindy Hudson.

I also had the help of a group of readers who reviewed the chapters for clarity even before they were submitted to the publisher: Guy Berger, Philip Cohen, Jeremy Falk, Mark Rabkin, Yaniv Soha, Ilan Spieler, and Mona, Jason, and Greg Reel. A special note of thanks to Eyal Soha, who reviewed every chapter and could be counted on to respond quickly when the deadlines seemed impossible.

I am deeply grateful to Franky Wong, who not only reviewed the book as it was being written, but carried much of the load of running Desaware while I worked on this project and others. Thanks also to Marian and Andy Kicklighter, Karyn Duncan, Stjepan Pejic, Alex Scherbakovsky, and my sister Roan Bear, who helped out and made sure that I took a break to eat and sleep at least once in a while.

A million thanks to my father, who also reviewed every chapter, and to my mother, whose book *Alicia: My Story* is still far more important to the world than mine could ever be (though I'm getting closer :-))...

Where do you live?

"Go down Hwy. 34 about three miles, take the Murphy's Law exit, turn right, then make a left just past the donut shop. It's the third house on the left."

When you give someone these directions, you have in essence created a "program" that they can use to get to your house. You are a programmer—even if you have never used a computer.

There are many myths about programming: that it is difficult and complex; that a programmer must be incredibly intelligent; that it takes years to learn. As with most myths, these do contain an element of truth. Some languages and systems *are* complex and demand substantial study to use effectively.

On the other hand, while one could spend a lifetime learning about cars, most people learn to drive in a few months. A professor of English literature can base an entire career on one literary movement or the works of a single author, yet any child can learn to read and write in a relatively short period of time. Likewise, programming does not require that you spend months and years learning particular programming languages or systems in order to grasp the fundamentals.

At a party with a friend a few years ago, I ran into an acquaintance who is also a programmer. We began to talk shop, and after a few moments my other friend drifted away. I later asked her why, and she explained that we had "stopped speaking English." Many of my friends have had similar experiences. Programmers often do speak a language seemingly all their own. You can even buy dictionaries of computer jargon; unfortunately, these books are usually not very effective. Like trying to learn a foreign language from a dictionary, just understanding the words is not enough to make one a programmer.

How Programming Works is not a dictionary of jargon. Nor does it try to teach you to program in a particular language. But by the time you have finished reading it, you will understand most of the concepts on which all computer programming and computer languages are based. When you actually start programming, whether in a high-level language or simply to program your microwave oven, you will know how to proceed—just as surely as you know that your microwave oven has a power level control somewhere, even if it takes a few minutes to find it and figure out how it works. After reading this book, when the conversation turns to computers and programming you will be able to follow it and participate—not because you have memorized lists of words, but because you will understand the *ideas* on which the conversation is based.

Perhaps you are already shaking your head in doubt at these promises. I can't blame you for being skeptical. All I ask is that you suspend your disbelief, at least for the first few chapters. I think you will be pleasantly surprised.

Programming skills are becoming more and more important. Even if you never write your own programs, today's computer applications are designed to be more programmable by you, the user. Most spreadsheets, word processors, and communications programs already contain built-in macro programming languages. Most modern video cassette recorders and high-end microwave ovens, as well as some games, are programmable.

If you are someone who finds computers (or even your VCR) frightening or intimidating, this book is for you. If you are a beginner and not sure where to begin, or you have been frustrated by other approaches, I think you will find some good direction here. Or perhaps you are a self-taught programmer who has never learned the fundamentals of the craft—here is your chance to find out what you've missed. And if you are a professional programmer, I hope you have as much fun reading this as I had writing it.

There's one more thing I'd like you to know before you start. It is perhaps the best-kept secret about computers and programming and is all too rarely mentioned: Programming is fun. Serious fun. I know many programmers who have privately admitted that they are lucky to have a programming job, because if they didn't, they would *pay for* the opportunity to do it instead of getting *paid to* program (but please don't tell their bosses!). One evening soon, you will start working on a project and suddenly realize that it is 3:00 a.m.—and you will know exactly what I mean.

Until then, remember one thing: You are already a programmer. This book is simply going to show you how to practice and apply skills that you already have.

If you have any comments about this book, I'd be delighted to hear from you. You can contact me via email at dan_appleman@apress.com

Daniel Appleman

GETTING STARTED

Chapter 1: What Are Hardware and Software?
4

Chapter 2: What Is a Computer Language?
10

OVERVIEW

COMPUTERS ARE DUMMIES; Hollywood has never realized this. If you watch almost any movie that features a computer, you will see that it is usually portrayed as intelligent and even malevolent. In the movie *2001*, HAL killed most of the crew on his mission. In *Star Wars* the 'droids C3PO and R2D2 had distinct personalities and were definitely intelligent. The entire Star Trek universe is populated by computers that respond intelligently to most questions, and the android Data sometimes seems more human than his crewmates.

This view of computers is often held by people who are working with computers for the first time. On the one hand, they feel intimidated by a machine that they think may be smarter than they are. On the other hand, they can't understand why the computer doesn't comprehend what they mean when they try to get it to do something.

The truth is, computers are dummies. Really, really, *really* stupid. It is almost impossible to overstate how incredibly dumb they are. The smartest computer ever made does not even have the intelligence of a newt. Computers can only react or respond to data or situations that a programmer has anticipated. The power of computers comes not from intelligence, but from speed. Modern computers can perform millions of simple operations each second. This speed, combined with clever software, often gives computers the illusion of intelligence.

Beginning programmers often expect computers to be smart, and get frustrated when the computer seems incapable of understanding the simplest commands. It is only after programmers realize computers are stupid that they really begin to make progress. In fact, a lot of programming consists of learning to think in a very simplistic and nit-picky manner.

When executing a program, the computer is incapable of making any judgments beyond those built in by the program designer. The computer will do exactly what the program tells it to. It has no discretion and no imagination. It's up to you as a programmer to bring yourself down to the computer's level, just as a parent might simplify instructions to a small child (except that any child capable of understanding instructions is already far more intelligent than your computer). The computer will always follow your instructions literally—just as a disobedient child might do to get on parents' nerves. Of course, unlike the child, the computer is not being deliberately disobedient—it really doesn't know any better.

What Are Hardware and Software?

WHEN YOU BEGIN a task on a computer, you are working with a machine that is made up of hardware and software. *Hardware* is that part of the machine that you can physically see and touch. It is built of metals, plastics, and tiny squares of silicon. *Software* is that part of the machine that you cannot see and touch. You can think of the combination of hardware and software as a book written in a foreign language. Hardware corresponds to the cover and pages of a book, and software corresponds to the actual contents of the book. But unless you know the language in which the book is written, the contents are impossible to understand. Only when you understand the language does the book take on meaning, conveying information or perhaps telling a story. The physical book itself is only the mechanism through which the story is communicated; it is the software that is the actual story. A computer without software is like a book with blank pages—it can't do anything. It is nothing more than an expensive doorstop.

Computers always have some built-in software. In most cases, this is a small program called a *monitor* or *BIOS*. It is usually just enough software to load other programs that make the computer actually work.

Programming is the process by which computer software is created, a process that is the subject of this book. You do not need to know a great deal about a computer's hardware in order to write software. Just as you can drive a car without understanding how a carburetor works, you can program a computer without knowing everything about how it functions. Still, it is useful to know a little bit about what is going on inside so that you can take greater advantage of the machine's capabilities.

Programming a Railroad

Without some procedure for setting the switches in a railroad yard, all activity is stopped cold. A computer works in much the same way as a railroad yard. Information arrives from the outside, is stored or processed, and then is sent on its way.

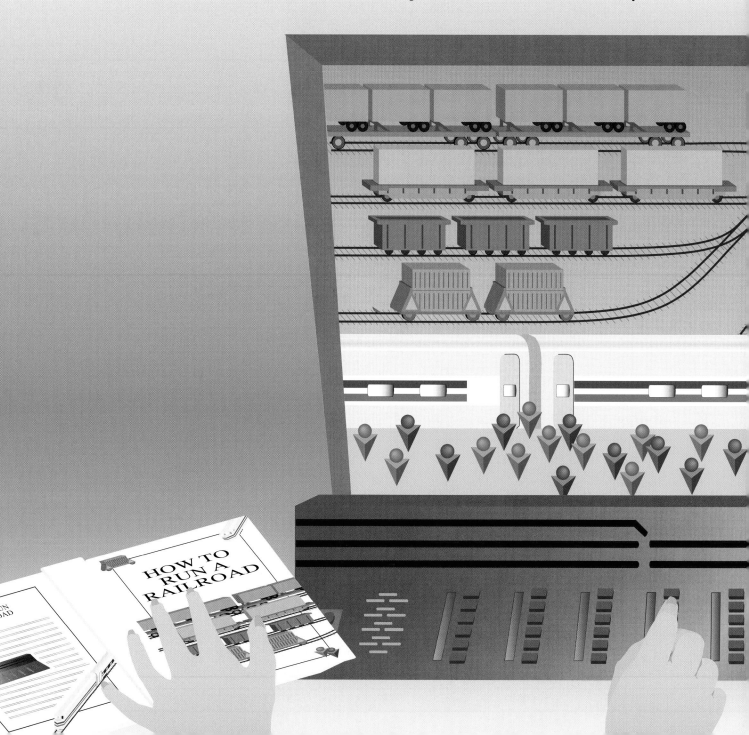

Inside the computer, hundreds of thousands of electronic switches control the information flow—but without some kind of procedure or "program," the computer is stopped.

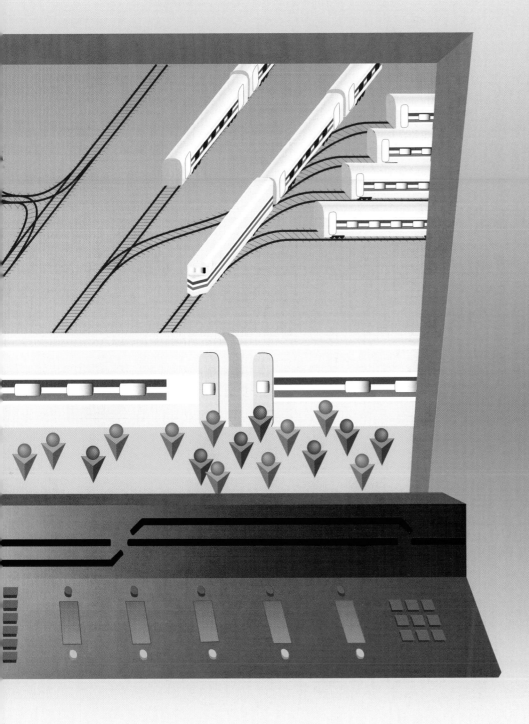

Information Flow

A computer will typically have hundreds of thousands, or even millions, of *transistor switches* that control the flow of information through the computer. The size of a switch in modern microcomputers is typically smaller than a few millionths of a square inch.

Long-term information storage is usually provided by disk drives or tape drives, which store data using magnetic recording in much the same way a cassette records music. Newer CD and DVD drives use materials that reflect light and are read using lasers

A computer can accept input from many sources. This information is stored internally in the form of numbers. No matter what kind of input is being processed, it must be converted into numbers before the computer can use it.

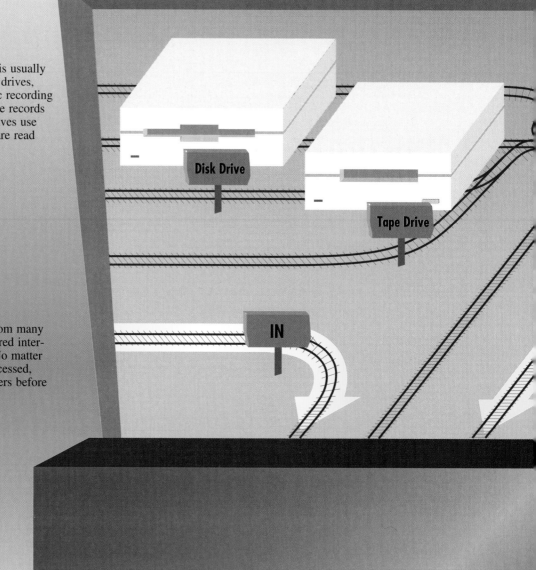

Many modern computers do not work alone. They are frequently connected to other machines, through either high-speed networks or slower serial ports and modems, which allow computers to talk to each other using standard phone lines. The term *I/O* stands for Input/Output and refers to every way in which a computer communicates with the outside world.

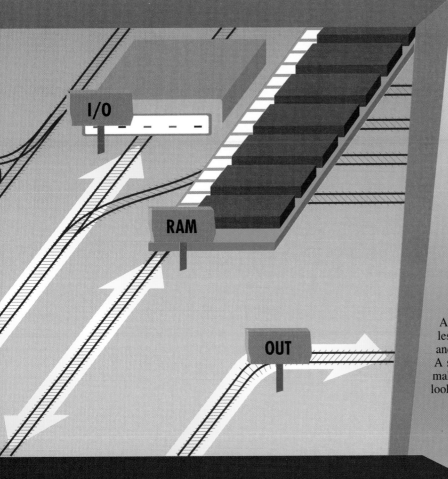

High-speed information storage is provided by high-speed random-access memory (RAM). This memory consists of millions of switches, which typically are arranged in groups of 8, 16, 32, or 64. The number of switches, or *bits*, in a group determines the size of the number that can be stored in that group. RAM is also used to store programs. At this level, a program consists of a series of numbers that the Central Processing Unit (CPU) can use to control other switches inside the computer. These numbers can be thought of as the most simple language, or *machine language*, of a computer.

All that information pouring into a computer is useless unless there is a way to get it out. Video screens and printers are the most common forms of output. A significant amount of programming effort goes into making the video display and printed output of data look good.

The Central Processing Unit (CPU) is the "yard master" of the computer. It controls the flow of data in the computer and performs operations on the data, as directed by the program that is running.

What Is a Computer Language?

PEOPLE USE MANY different forms of language to communicate. Languages can be written, read, spoken, heard, and even signed. There are special languages that allow people to communicate with computers, because computers are not capable of understanding human languages. Human languages tend to be quite sophisticated. Punctuation and phrasing can change the meaning of a sentence. Consider the following ambiguous sentence: "The car drove away quickly." Did the car leave as soon as possible, or did it leave at high speed? Or how about: "Help wild horses." Look how the meaning changes when it is punctuated: "Help! Wild horses!" Humans, being intelligent, are able to interpret subtle changes in inflection and punctuation. Computers, being stupid, do not have this ability.

Modern computer languages use words from human languages, have rules of grammar, syntax, and punctuation, and often read vaguely like human languages. However, they actually are very limited and specialized. Since a computer does not have understanding, computer languages are designed to be unambiguous. Computer languages also are simpler than human languages. A human language typically has hundreds of thousands of words. Computer languages can have as few as a couple of dozen words, and rarely have more than a few hundred. Generally speaking, computer languages demand a great deal of precision on the part of a programmer. Human beings can often interpret ambiguous statements, but even a small error in punctuation or a typographical error in a computer program can cause an entire program to fail.

Computers understand only sequences of numbers. Ultimately, the purpose of any computer language is to translate your commands into numbers that can be interpreted by computer hardware. Computer languages are themselves programs, and like any program, can vary in capability and complexity. Low-level languages such as Assembly Language allow direct access to all of the capabilities of the underlying hardware. However, these langauages can make programming difficult and time consuming. Higher level languages such as C++, BASIC, and Java make programming easier by hiding many of the low-level details of the hardware, and by combining many low-level commands into more powerful language statements. Programmers are working to create language programs that are capable of understanding human languages, and have achieved some degree of success, but they still have a long way to go.

Programming a Turtle

Imagine you could create a drawing by tying a pen to the tail of a turtle and giving the turtle directions on which path to take. The turtle would need to understand a language that contained a few simple commands, such as Forward, Left, Right, PenUp, PenDown. Now imagine a computer language with the same commands that could control a turtle on a computer screen. There is such a language: It's called LOGO, and it contains a group of graphics commands called Turtle Graphics. This language is used to teach programming to young children, but make no mistake—it is a full-featured and powerful language, indeed.

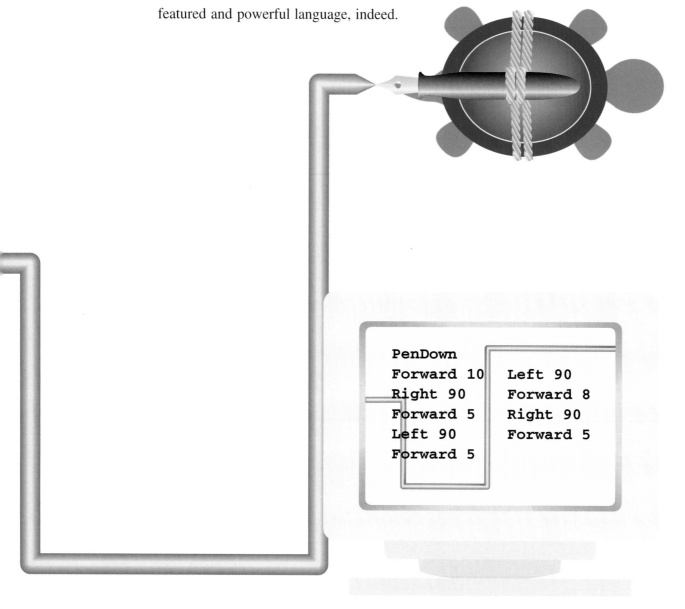

```
PenDown
Forward 10     Left 90
Right 90       Forward 8
Forward 5      Right 90
Left 90        Forward 5
Forward 5
```

1 In LOGO, Forward moves the turtle forward, and Left and Right turn the turtle by the number of degrees specified. PenUp and PenDown lift or drop the pen. If the pen is up, you can move the turtle without drawing. You can draw a box as shown on the screen to the left.

```
To Box
>PenDown       >Right 90
>Forward 10    >Forward 10
>Right 90      >Right 90
>Forward 10    >PenUp
>Right 90      >End
>Forward 10    BOX
```

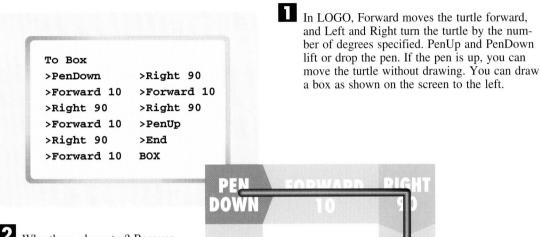

2 Why the > character? Because the first statement 'To' told LOGO to record the commands under the name *Box*. The > indicates that the command is being recorded instead of executed immediately. The End statement told LOGO to stop recording the commands. Now, any time you type *Box*, the turtle will draw a box.

```
Box
Right 45
PenColor 2
Box
Right 45
PenColor 5
Box
```

3 This is a very simple LOGO program that can be used to draw lots of boxes easily. We can use the PenColor command to change the color of the pen, as well.

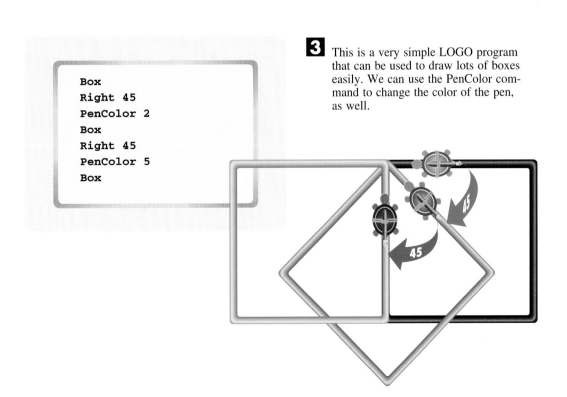

A Hierarchy of Languages

1 Most programmers use high-level languages such as C++, BASIC, and Java. These languages hide the details of the particular computer from the programmer, letting him or her work with commands and data provided by the language itself instead of worrying about a particular machine language or memory organization. This makes it possible to create programs that will run on many different computers. A program called a *compiler* or *interpreter* is used to convert a program in a high-level language into the machine language for a particular computer. One line in a high-level language might be converted into dozens of lines of machine language.

2 Before high-level languages were invented, programmers created a very simple language in which each command represents the numbers of individual machine-language commands. This is called an *assembly language*. A program called an *assembler* converts the assembly-language text into the numbers that the computer can use.

3 A computer represents all information internally in the form of numbers. This includes programs. The numbers that make up a program that the computer hardware is able to use directly are in the machine language of the computer. In the early days of computing, people would actually program in machine language, using switches or punch cards to enter the machine-language program directly into memory.

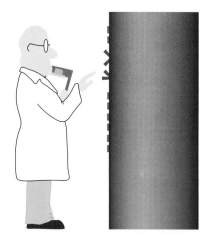

4 In this example, you have a simple program in the C language that draws a box. It is translated first into assembly language, and then into the machine language. This particular example was written for use with the Microsoft Windows operating environment. The assembly language and machine language shown is that for the Intel family of microprocessors. The numbers shown in the machine language screen are in base 16, also known as hexadecimal. You'll read more about that later. As you can see, the higher level C language is quite easy to understand, the assembly-language code is considerably more cryptic, and the machine language is meaningless to the casual reader. This demonstrates one of the major advantages of a high-level language.

```c
VOID EXPORTAPI DrawBox(HDC hdc)
{
// hdc is a value used by Windows to identify a
// window to draw in.
// The numbers represent coordinates in the window.
   MoveTo(hdc, 50,50);
   LineTo(hdc, 100,50);
   LineTo(hdc, 100,100);
   LineTo(hdc, 50,100);
   LineTo(hdc, 50,50);
   }
```

```
DrawBox:                                  push   OFFSET 100
   mov   ax,SEG con0                      push   OFFSET 100
   enter OFFSET L08041,OFFSET 0           call   FAR PTR LineTo
   push  si                               push   WORD PTR 6[bp]
   push  di                               push   OFFSET 50
   push  ds                               push   OFFSET 100
   mov   ds,ax                            call   FAR PTR LineTo
   push  WORD PTR 6[bp]                   push   WORD PTR 6[bp]
   push  OFFSET 50                        push   OFFSET 50
   push  OFFSET 50                        push   OFFSET 50
   call  FAR PTR MoveTo                   call   FAR PTR LineTo
   push  WORD PTR 6[bp]                   pop    ds
   push  OFFSET 100                       pop    di
   push  OFFSET 50                        pop    si
   call  FAR PTR LineTo                   leave
   push  WORD PTR 6[bp]                   ret    OFFSET 2
```

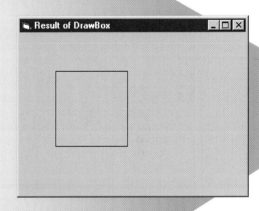

```
B8 87 55              6A 64
C8 02 00 00           9A 96 0E 0F 05
56                    FF 76 06
57                    6A 32
1E                    6A 64
8E D8                 9A 96 0E 0F 05
FF 76 06              FF 76 06
6A 32                 6A 32
6A 32                 6A 32
9A AA 0E 0F 05        9A 96 0E 0F 05
FF 76 06              E9 00 00
6A 64                 1F
6A 32                 5F
9A 96 0E 0F 05        5E
FF 76 06              C9
6A 64                 CA 02 00
```

Even though they are using the same computer hardware, each of these programmers perceives the machine differently. We call the machine that they perceive a "virtual machine." For example, when you use a word processor on a computer, you don't worry about the language in which the word processing program was written—all you care about is that it handle your text correctly. Thus, the "virtual machine" that you see is a word processor.

DATA

Chapter 3: Variables
20

Chapter 4: Numeric Variables
26

Chapter 5: Text Variables
30

Chapter 6: Boolean and Flag Variables
36

Chapter 7: Pointers
44

TAKE A MOMENT and think about some of the things that computer programs do. Money-management programs can print checks and balance checkbooks. Word processing programs allow you to type and edit text, format and print papers, and even check your spelling. Video games allow you to shoot down alien spacecraft or fly a software-generated airplane. The possibilities are endless, yet all programs have one thing in common: They manipulate data.

When learning a computer language, it is tempting to want to learn first about the commands that a language provides. But commands that manipulate data are not particularly useful until you know something about how the data itself is handled by the language. For example, every computer language must provide a way to store data. *Variables* serve this purpose by providing a mechanism for identifying each item of data using a descriptive name. As you will see, variables come in many types, shapes, and sizes. Not every type of variable can be found in every language, and some languages are better at handling certain types than others, but every language has variables in one form or another.

The first part of learning any language is to find out what types of variables it supports, and how to use them. The following chapters describe the types of variables that you are most likely to run into, regardless of which language you choose to work with.

Variables

TAKE A DOLLAR out of your pocket and examine it. It's nothing more than a piece of paper—green and black with a lot of complex patterns. How can it have value? The paper you are examining is a symbol. It represents a unit of value that we have agreed to call "one dollar." Humans make use of symbols all the time to represent real objects, so it should be no surprise that computer languages are designed to use the same technique when working with data.

You already know that the data your program uses is stored in variables. Perhaps you don't know that each variable has a name you assign to it. This name represents the data in much the same way a dollar bill represents a unit of currency. When you name variables, it is a good idea to choose a name that fits the meaning of a variable. For example, if you are using a variable to hold the number of videotapes that you own, you might want to call it "VideoTapesOwned." Defining variables—assigning them their names and meanings—is one of the first tasks in designing any program. This process is called *declaring* variables.

A computer saves data internally in the form of numbers. The programmer uses a computer language to give these numbers meaning. Consider a variable name "Cars" that contains the number 5. The language itself understands only the number. The programmer interprets this number to mean a number of vehicles. Some languages provide special named variables that have a constant value. For example, the constant variable named "PI" might have the value 3.141593. A variable also has a location, or *address*, in the computer's memory, but in most cases the computer language itself takes care of locating the variable in memory.

Computer languages support many types of variables. The most common of these are numeric variables and text variables. But many languages also support date variables, currency variables, and user-defined variables.

Variables: The Mailboxes of a Computer Program

Variables are the mailboxes of a computer program. Each variable contains data, just as a mailbox contains letters. Each variable has an address, just as each mailbox is assigned a street address. Finally, each variable has a name, just as mailboxes are labeled with the name of a company or family.

2 When you mail a letter to Joe, you look up Joe's address in your address book. The postal service uses that address to find the mailbox for the letter. To save data in a variable, you specify the name of the variable. Your computer language then looks up the address for the variable and stores the data in the addressed location in memory.

Joe Variable
35 Memory Lane
Computerville, USA

1 A computer's memory consists of a sequence of locations, each of which is identified by an address. When you define a variable, the language assigns it a location in memory that will hold the data that you place in the variable. While some languages allow you to refer to a variable by its address, in most cases you will refer to the variable by the name you give it.

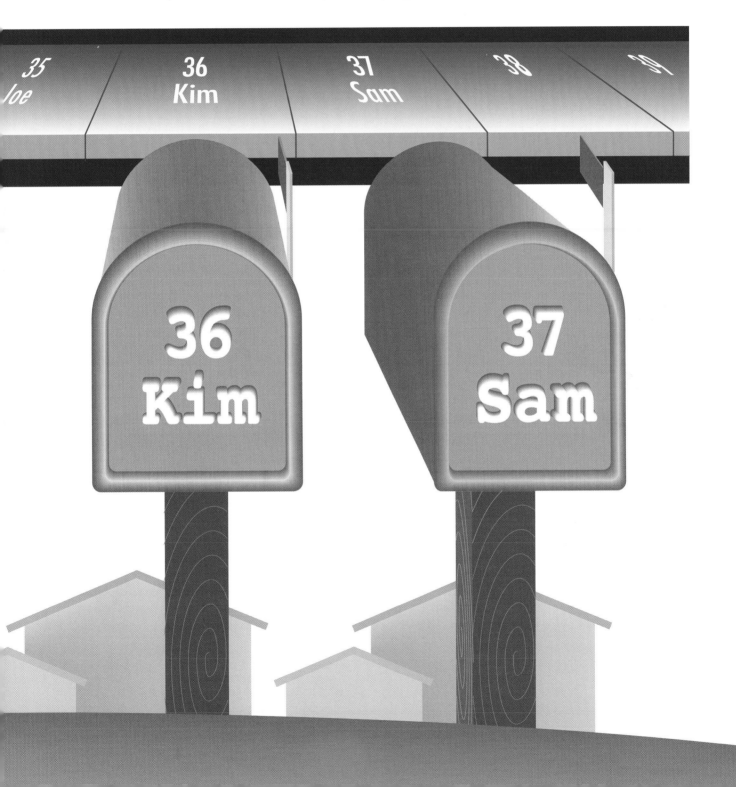

Specialized Variables

Imagine if individual mailboxes held only one type of mail. One could hold only bills, another only magazines, and another only junk mail. Program variables are specialized in this way. A computer language provides many different types of variables, each with its own characteristics. Many languages allow you to define new variable types, as well.

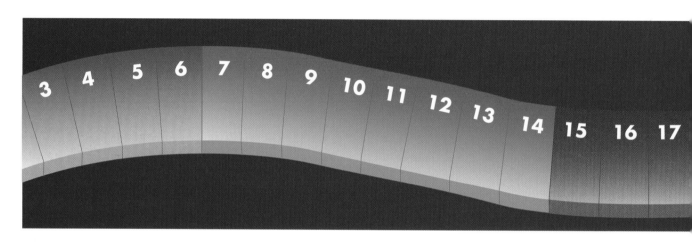

A currency variable is a fixed-point decimal number with two or four positions to the right of the decimal point. Example: $35.26

A text variable contains one or more characters. Example: "Hello"

Each type of variable takes up a different amount of space in the computer's memory. The address of a variable is considered to be the location in memory where the variable begins.

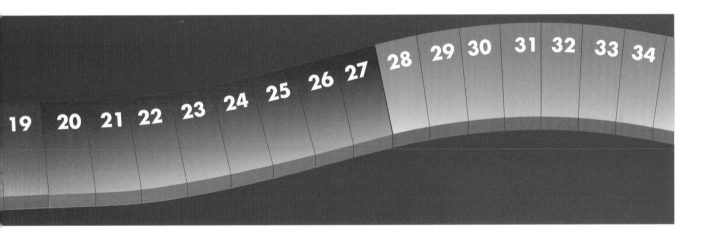

Real numbers are used to hold very small or very large values—for example, those used to measure astronomical distances. Example: 1.86×10^6

User-defined variables can be almost any size, and can be made up of variables of other types. You'll find out more about user-defined variables in Part 4.

Numeric Values

NUMBERS ARE THE most common type of data that computer programs use. This is obvious in some cases. For example, programs that perform financial or scientific calculations use numeric variables extensively. But this is also true for applications that appear to deal mostly with text. A word processor may use text variables for the text itself. But you can see that there are many numeric variables that the program uses behind the scenes to calculate the size and position of each sentence and letter in a document.

In math class, we are taught about two general categories of numbers: real numbers and integers. Real numbers can have a fractional part—digits to the right of a decimal point. They can take on any value and can be as accurate as you wish-and you can add as many digits to the right of the decimal point as you need. Integers are whole numbers without a fractional part, such as 1, 3, 1000, −5, etc. They can range from 0 to infinity (positive or negative).

In computer programs, numbers are represented by combinations of bits of memory that typically are 8, 16, or 32 bits wide. The number of bits determines the largest number that can be represented by each group. Different computers have different capabilities when it comes to combining these groups to form larger numbers and when working directly with real numbers. It is the job of the language itself to translate the variables you use into the right form for storage in the computer's memory and the operations you specify into operations that the computer can execute.

Most computer languages provide a wide selection of numeric variable types that include both integer types and real types. Your job as a programmer is to decide which type of variable to use to represent the different data in your program. Each type has different characteristics.

Range specifies the minimum and maximum value that a numeric variable can hold. *Resolution* specifies the number of possible values that a numeric variable can hold. In real numbers, resolution specifies the number of significant figures that the variable can hold without losing accuracy. Numeric variables also can be signed or unsigned—this determines whether the variable can hold negative numbers. The type of variable also determines the time it takes to perform operations on the data contained in the variable.

Types of Numeric Variables

Computer memory is organized into groups of switches, or bits. A bit can take the value 0 or 1, depending on the state of the switch. Variables are built of one or more of these groups. The characteristics of the variable are determined by the number of bits it contains.

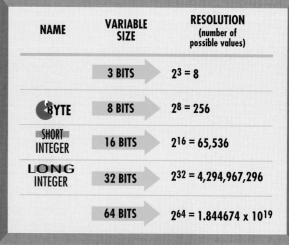

NAME	VARIABLE SIZE	RESOLUTION (number of possible values)
	3 BITS	$2^3 = 8$
BYTE	8 BITS	$2^8 = 256$
SHORT INTEGER	16 BITS	$2^{16} = 65,536$
LONG INTEGER	32 BITS	$2^{32} = 4,294,967,296$
	64 BITS	$2^{64} = 1.844674 \times 10^{19}$

Range and Resolution
   Example: A variable made of 3 bits

Switch States								
Bit Values	000	001	010	011	100	101	110	111
Decimal Value	0	1	2	3	4	5	6	7

Each variable has a fixed number of possible values, but there is no requirement that all variables be positive. By using the leftmost (high-order) bit as a *sign bit*, it is possible to shift the range such that half of the numbers are negative. The number lines below demonstrate how this is accomplished.

0	1	2	3	4	5	6	7
000	001	010	011	100	101	110	111
-4	-3	-2	-1	0	1	2	3
100	101	110	111	000	001	010	011

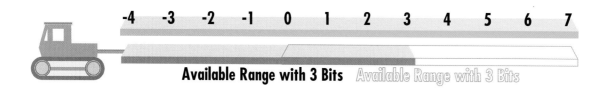

Available Range with 3 Bits

Common Numeric Types

Variable Type	Number of Bits	Range	Resolution	Typical Application	Performance
BYTE	8	0 to 255 (unsigned) −128 to 127 (signed)	256	characters, enumerated values (such as lists of colors), image processing	Very fast.
SHORT INTEGER	16	0 to 65535 (unsigned) −32768 to 32767 (signed)	65536	counters, miscellaneous numbers	Very fast on 16-bit and 32- bit computers. Slower on others.
LONG INTEGER	32	0 to 2^{32} (unsigned) $−2^{31}$ to $2^{31}−1$ (signed)	2^{32}	very large numbers	Very fast on 32-bit computers. Slower on others.
CURRENCY	64	$−9.22 \times 10^{14}$ to 9.22×10^{14}	2^{64} (19 significant digits)	currency	Intermediate.
FLOAT FLOAT	32	1.40×10^{-45} to 3.40×10^{38} (positive) $−1.40 \times 10^{-45}$ to $−3.40 \times 10^{38}$	7 significant digits	science, mathematics, currency	Slow. Faster with hardware accelerators.
DOUBLE DOUBLE	64	4.94×10^{-134} to 4.94×10^{308} (positive) $−4.94 \times 10^{-134}$ to $−4.94 \times 10^{308}$	15 significant digits	science, mathematics, currency	Slow. Faster with hardware accelerators.

Remember, not all languages support all these types.

Equivalent Variable Types

Variable Type	Variable Type in Visual Basic	Variable Type in C or C++
BYTE	Byte	char, unsigned char
SHORT INTEGER	integer (signed only)	short, unsigned short
LONG INTEGER	long (signed only)	long, unsigned long
CURRENCY	currency	no equivalent
FLOAT FLOAT	single	single
DOUBLE DOUBLE	double	double

C also has a type called *int*, which can be 16 or 32 bits, depending on the individual language implementation.

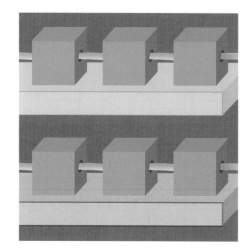

Text Variables

YOU CAN FIND text in reports, on screen prompts, in spreadsheets and databases, and, of course, in word-processed documents. You will also find text in every computer program. It is not surprising, therefore, that computer languages provide variables designed to handle text information.

As mentioned earlier, all data a computer uses must be represented internally by numbers, so it is necessary to assign a number, or code, to each text character in order for a computer to work with text information. Perhaps you made up a secret code when you were younger. Consider the following example of a simple code: A = 1, B = 2, C = 3, and so on through Z = 26. Using this code, the title of the book you are reading now (not counting the spaces between words) would be represented as: 8 15 23 16 18 15 7 18 1 13 13 9 14 7 23 15 18 11 19. This particular code is limited because it handles only capital letters of the Roman alphabet. Even the simplest character code for computers not only has to hold uppercase letters, but also lowercase letters, punctuation, and special control codes such as the line feed code, which indicates the start of a new line.

A computer code has one other requirement in addition to handling many types of characters. It has to be a standard. If each computer used a different code, it would be impossible for computers to exchange information or share text files. IBM pioneered a standard code called EBCDIC, but the most common code used today is a 7-bit code known as *ASCII* (American Standard Code for Information Interchange). This code allows each character to be stored efficiently in a single 8-bit byte.

ASCII has one major limitation: It stores only a maximum of 127 characters. This limit is adequate for English, but it cannot accommodate all the characters used by every language in the world. Even extended ASCII, which uses 8 bits to represent up to 255 characters, is not adequate for this task. Another code, called *Unicode*, is used on newer advanced operating systems. Unicode uses 16 bits to represent up to 65,535 possible charactersómore than enough to handle every alphabet.

ASCII: The Not-So-Secret Code

There are some cases where text needs to be converted into a truly secret numeric code—a process called *encryption*. Secret agents encrypt their messages so that they canít be read by enemy agents. But even at the height of the Cold War, any spy who brought in a nonstandard computer code for general use that handled only letters would have been laughed at...or worse.

The first 31 characters of the ASCII code are control characters, which were needed to control hardware—specifically teletype machines that are no longer used. Some of these codes are still used by terminal programs and within text files. The lower table shows the numeric value of each character in decimal and hexadecimal, the name of the control character, and a description for those that are in common use today; the upper table lists printable characters. (See the illustration "Casting a Hex: Flags, Booleans, and Masks," in the next chapter, for details on the decimal and hexadecimal number systems.)

NOT SECR
FOR EVERY SYSTEM

ASCII

9 = 57	? = 63
: = 58	@ = 64
; = 59	A = 65
< = 60	B = 66
= = 61	C = 67
> = 62	D = 68
	E = 69

Here lies
EBCDIC
Electronic Binary
Coded Decimal
Interchange Code
"We used to use it.
Now we don't"

OP SECRET
FOR YOUR SYSTEM ONLY

The ASCII Code
Printable Characters

Dec	Hex	Char	Dec	Hex	Char	Dec	Hex	Char	Dec	Hex	Char
32	20	Space	56	38	8	80	50	P	104	68	h
33	21	!	57	39	9	81	51	Q	105	69	i
34	22	"	58	3A	:	82	52	R	106	6A	j
35	23	#	59	3B	;	83	53	S	107	6B	k
36	24	$	60	3C	<	84	54	T	108	6C	l
37	25	%	61	3D	=	85	55	U	109	6D	m
38	26	&	62	3E	>	86	56	V	110	6E	n
39	27	'	63	3F	?	87	57	W	111	6F	o
40	28	(	64	40	@	88	58	X	112	70	p
41	29	)	65	41	A	89	59	Y	113	71	q
42	2A	*	66	42	B	90	5A	Z	114	72	r
43	2B	+	67	43	C	91	5B	[	115	73	s
44	2C	,	68	44	D	92	5C	\	116	74	t
45	2D	-	69	45	E	93	5D	]	117	75	u
46	2E	.	70	46	F	94	5E	^	118	76	v
47	2F	/	71	47	G	95	5F	_	119	77	w
48	30	0	72	48	H	96	60	`	120	78	x
49	31	1	73	49	I	97	61	a	121	79	y
50	32	2	74	4A	J	98	62	b	122	7A	z
51	33	3	75	4B	K	99	63	c	123	7B	{
52	34	4	76	4C	L	100	64	d	124	7C		
53	35	5	77	4D	M	101	65	e	125	7D	}
54	36	6	78	4E	N	102	66	f	126	7E	~
55	37	7	79	4F	O	103	67	g	127	7F	Del

The ASCII Code
Control Characters

Dec	Hex	Char	Description
0	00	NUL	Null character. In the C language, used to mark the end of a string.
1	01	SOH	Start of heading
2	02	STX	Start of text
3	03	ETX	The ^C character. Often used to stop transmission of a text block via modem.
4	04	EOT	End of Text
5	05	ENQ	Enquiry
6	06	ACK	Acknowledge
7	07	BEL	Sounds a beep on many terminals.
8	08	BS	The backspace character.
9	09	HT	The tab character.
10	0A	LF	The line feed character. Marks the start of a new line.
11	0B	VT	Vertical tab
12	0C	FF	The form feed character. Marks the start of a new page. Performs a page eject on many printers.
13	0D	CR	The carriage return character. Returns the print location to the left margin.
14	0E	SO	Shift out
15	0F	SI	Shift in
16	10	DLE	Data link escape
17	11	DC1	The ^Q character. Often used to restart modem communication paused using the ^S character.
18	12	DC2	Device control 2
19	13	DC3	The ^S character. Often used to pause modem communication.
20	14	DC4	Device control 4
21	15	NAK	Negative acknowledge
22	16	SYN	Synchronous idle
23	17	ETB	End transmission block
24	18	CAN	Cancel
25	19	EM	End of medium
26	1A	SUB	The ^Z character. Sometimes used to mark the end of a text file.
27	1B	ESC	The Escape character. Often used to cancel an operation.
28	1C	FS	File separator
29	1D	GS	Group separator
30	1E	RS	Record separator
31	1F	US	Unit separator

Text Variables

Text variables are often called strings due to their ability to string together characters. Each character is stored internally as an ASCII code number.

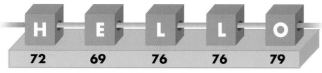

Converting to and from ASCII

Each language provides a way to obtain the ASCII value for a character, or set a character from an ASCII value. This makes it easy for a program to perform complex operations on text. For example: To convert an uppercase character to lowercase, all you need to do is obtain the ASCII value of the character, add 32, and set the character with the resulting ASCII value. Text comparisons, sorting, and searching also rely on the numeric ASCII values of text strings.

```
Dim AsciiValue As Integer
Dim StringVarible As String

AsciiValue = Asc (StringVariable)
'Get the ASCII value of the first
'character in string StringVariable

StringVariable = Chr$(AsciiValue)
'StringVariable is set to a string with
'a single character whose ASCII code
'is AsciiValue.
```

Representing Numbers As Strings

Sometimes, people confuse a numeric variable that contains a number and a text variable that contains a text representation of that number. In this example, the number 1,452 can be stored in a 16-bit integer variable or as the character string 1452, which is 4 bytes long.

1,452

1,452 as a number

`0 0 0 0 0 1 0 1 1 0 1 0 1 1 0 0`

HIGH BYTE   **LOW BYTE**

1,452 as a string

`1   4   5   2`

ASCII Code

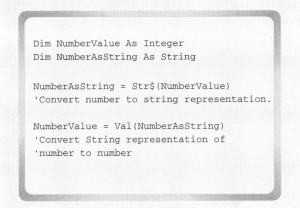

```
Dim NumberValue As Integer
Dim NumberAsString As String


NumberAsString = Str$(NumberValue)
'Convert number to string representation.


NumberValue = Val(NumberAsString)
'Convert String representation of
'number to number
```

Converting between Strings and Integers

Each language provides a way to obtain the string representation of a number and to convert that representation into a numeric variable. You will often convert numbers into strings when they need to be included in a block of textófor example, the number in an address. You will typically convert strings into numbers when you need to perform mathematical calculations on the number.

Inside a String

For many languages, such as BASIC, the internal format of a string variable is of no concern to the programmer. The language takes care of locating the variable in memory and performing any necessary operations on the string. Other languages allow the programmer to work directly with the memory containing the string. In these cases, it is useful to know how the string is stored in memory. In some versions of BASIC and Pascal, the first 16 or 32 bits of the storage space allocated to the string contain its length. In the C language, a string is a sequence of characters that is ended by a NULL character (ASCII value 0). The disadvantage of the C approach is that a string cannot contain the NULL character. In all of these cases, a mechanism exists for the language to determine the length of a string.

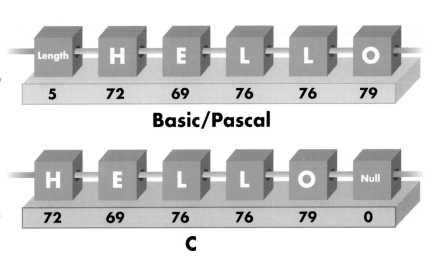

Character Sets

An 8-bit byte can contain up to 256 possible character values. This is fine for English, but leads to problems for programs that need to work with other languages or with large numbers of special symbols. For example, the Japanese alphabet alone (not including punctuation and so on) cannot fit into 256 characters. For many languages or symbol sets, it is possible to use different sets of characters beyond those defined by straight ASCII, especially when it comes to characters 128 through 255. These alternate character sets are often called *Code Pages*.

A Better Way—Unicode

A more long-term solution is a replacement for ASCII called Unicode, which is being promoted by many operating system vendors including Microsoft in its more advanced operating systems such as NT and Windows 2000. Unicode uses 16 bits for each character, allowing it to represent up to 65,535 characters. You can read more about Unicode at http://www.unicode.org.

Boolean and Flag Variables

ACCORDING TO SHAKESPEARE, Hamlet has two choices: *to be* or *not to be*. You could represent these choices with a single switch: ON = to be, OFF = not to be. Computers contain millions of switches, so it should be no surprise that computers are very good at handling situations where there are only two choices. This is important, because programs make choices. In some cases, a program may prompt a user for a yes or no answer. In other cases, a program may perform different operations, depending on the results of a calculation.

Most people are well acquainted with the kinds of operations that work on numbers: addition, subtraction, multiplication, division, and so on. Computer languages provide a special set of operations that work on variables that represent choices. These operations are called logical, or *Boolean*, operations after George Boole, a mathematician who defined them in the mid-1800s. Boolean operations include AND, OR, NOT, and XOR (Exclusive OR). A *truth table* shows the result of a Boolean operation for every possible combination of values. The branch of mathematics that uses these logical operations is called Boolean algebra.

Some computer languages provide special Boolean variables that can take on only two values: TRUE or FALSE. Most languages use numeric variables to represent these choices. In almost all cases, the value FALSE is defined as the number zero, and the value TRUE is defined as anything other than zero.

A Boolean value can be represented as a single bit, but for reasons of performance, a program will usually use an integer for this purpose. However, there are two cases where individual bits are used as Boolean values. The first is when it is necessary to conserve space—you can pack up to eight Boolean values into a single 8-bit byte. The other is when you are reading data from a hardware device such as an I/O port or a graphic card. These devices frequently use individual bits in a byte to return information. You can use Boolean operations to retrieve and set individual bits in these situations.

A Boolean variable that is used in a program to indicate a specific condition is also frequently called a *flag*.

The Philosophy of Booleans

The ancient Greeks pioneered the use of logic in discussion. These arguments can be represented in Boolean algebra as equations, with the Boolean variables shown in italics. While it is unlikely that the Greek philosophers discussed such mundane concerns as home-security systems, if they had, their conversation might have gone something like this:

If the front door is open or the front window is open, then sound the alarm.

SoundAlarm = *FrontDoorOpen* OR *FrontWindowOpen*

I see, but what about the side window?
If the side window is open or the side door is open, and the front door isn't open and the motion detector is triggered, then sound the alarm.

SoundAlarm = (*SideWindowOpen* OR *SideDoorOpen*) AND (*NOT FrontDoorOpen*) AND *MotionDetect*

AND

Variable A	Variable B	Variable A AND Variable B
False	False	False
False	True	False
True	False	False
True	True	True

Combining two Boolean variables with AND returns TRUE if both variables are TRUE.

OR

Variable A	Variable B	Variable A OR Variable B
False	False	False
False	True	True
True	False	True
True	True	True

Combining two Boolean variables with OR returns TRUE if either variable is TRUE.

A Boolean variable represents a choice between two possible values. These values can have many names, depending on the program and language used. Here are the most common:

TRUE:
1, –1, Nonzero, Yes, On, Logic High

FALSE:
0, No, Off, Stop, Logic Low

Nonsense!
If the front door is open and the motion detector is triggered, but the back door isn't open, then sound the alarm.

SoundAlarm = (*FrontDoorOpen* AND *MotionDetect*)
AND NOT *BackDoorOpen*

Too complex. Try this: If the front door is open and the side window isn't open, or the front door isn't open and the side window is open, then sound the alarm.

SoundAlarm = (*FrontDoorOpen* XOR *SideWindowOpen*)

XOR

Variable A	Variable B	Variable A XOR Variable B
False	False	False
False	True	True
True	False	True
True	True	False

Combining two Boolean variables with XOR returns TRUE only if one of the variables is TRUE.

NOT

Variable A	NOT Variable A
False	True
True	False

The NOT operator returns TRUE if the variable is FALSE, TRUE otherwise.

Flags:
A Sometimes Alarming Concept

A typical modern home alarm system has a large number of switches that detect various conditions in the house. Each switch has a wire to a central controller. The controller contains a small computer that runs a home-security program that constantly monitors the signals on these wires. The computer uses Boolean algebra to determine the conditions under which the alarm should be sounded. It is up to the programmer to act the part of the philosopher and define these logical equations. Once defined, the program can use them to sound the alarm when necessary.

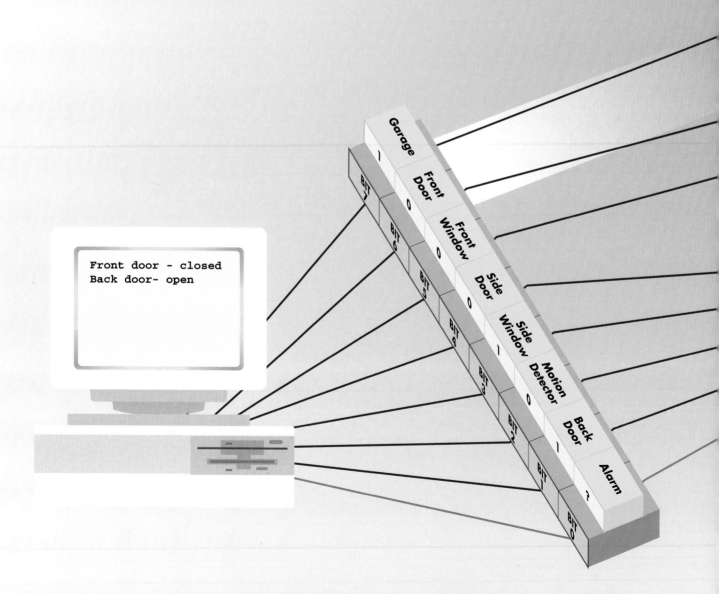

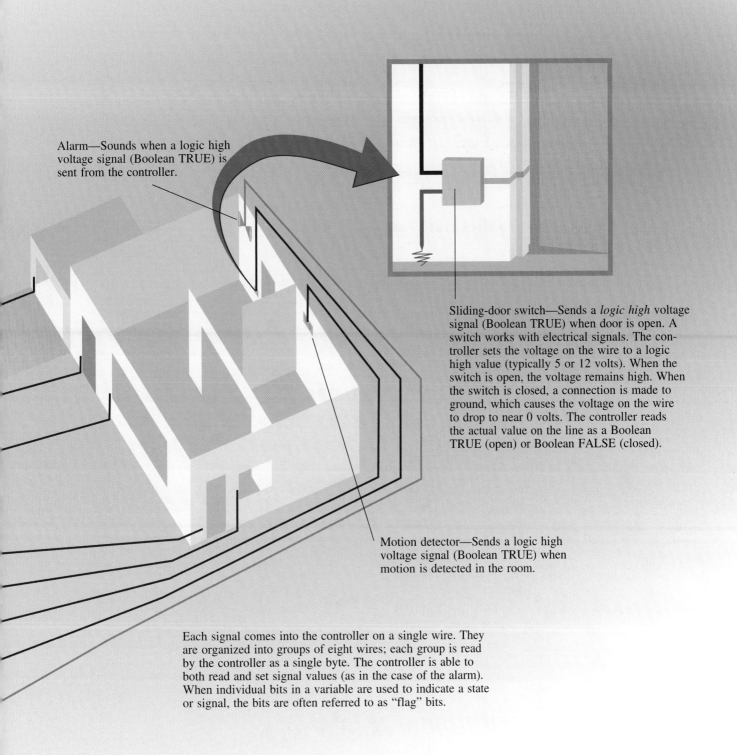

Alarm—Sounds when a logic high voltage signal (Boolean TRUE) is sent from the controller.

Sliding-door switch—Sends a *logic high* voltage signal (Boolean TRUE) when door is open. A switch works with electrical signals. The controller sets the voltage on the wire to a logic high value (typically 5 or 12 volts). When the switch is open, the voltage remains high. When the switch is closed, a connection is made to ground, which causes the voltage on the wire to drop to near 0 volts. The controller reads the actual value on the line as a Boolean TRUE (open) or Boolean FALSE (closed).

Motion detector—Sends a logic high voltage signal (Boolean TRUE) when motion is detected in the room.

Each signal comes into the controller on a single wire. They are organized into groups of eight wires; each group is read by the controller as a single byte. The controller is able to both read and set signal values (as in the case of the alarm). When individual bits in a variable are used to indicate a state or signal, the bits are often referred to as "flag" bits.

Casting a Hex: Flags, Booleans, and Masks

Since individual bits are often used as Boolean values, it is useful to know how to work with individual bits in a byte. Performing operations on individual bits requires that you understand two concepts: how to use the Boolean operations, and how to determine the numeric value of a byte when a single bit is set.

Hexadecimal

1 The number system that we all use is called the *decimal* system. The rightmost digit counts ones, the next digit counts tens, and so on. If we had 16 fingers instead of ten, we would probably use base 16, a number system called *hexadecimal*.

Binary	Decimal	Hex
0000	0	0
0001	1	1
0010	2	2
0011	3	3
0100	4	4
0101	5	5
0110	6	6
0111	7	7
1000	8	8
1001	9	9
1010	10	A
1011	11	B
1100	12	C
1101	13	D
1110	14	E
1111	15	F

2 In hexadecimal, the rightmost digit counts ones, the next digit counts 16s, and the next digit counts 256s. Because each digit has 16 possible values, the digits 0 through 9 are not enough. We use letters A through F to represent 10 through 15.

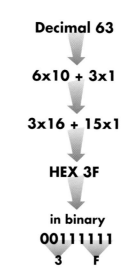

0 - F
16's

0 - F
1's

| 7 | 6 | 5 | 4 | 3 | 2 | 1 | 0 | Bit Number |

Decimal 63

6x10 + 3x1

3x16 + 15x1

HEX 3F

in binary
00111111
3   F

3 Why use hexadecimal? Because each digit takes up exactly 4 bits in the computer. Since we know the exact bit pattern for each "hex" digit, it becomes extremely easy to determine the values of each bit in a hexadecimal number, or to determine the hexadecimal value for a particular bit pattern. Programmers who work in assembly language or who write programs for controllers (such as home-alarm systems) frequently learn to think in hexadecimal as easily as you or I think in the decimal system.

Masks

At a masquerade party, a mask works by letting you see only a portion of a person's face. You can use Boolean operations in much the same way to access individual bits in a variable. A variable that is created in order to perform operations on individual bits in a variable is called a *mask variable*.

Retrieving a Single Bit in a Byte

When you perform a Boolean operation on two bytes, the operation is applied to each pair of bits. For example, if you perform a Boolean AND operation on a variable to be tested and on a mask variable, the resulting value will have a 1 only in the bit positions that were set to 1 both in the variable and in the mask. The AND operation is applied to each bit position of the two variables. You can retrieve the value of a single bit in a variable by setting a 1 in the corresponding bit position in the mask variable, and setting all of the other bits in the mask to 0.

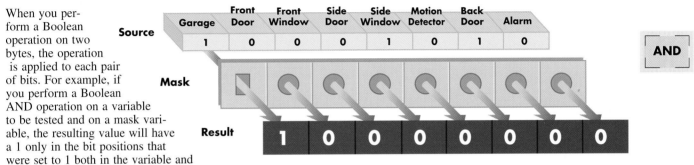

Clearing Individual Bits in a Byte

The Boolean AND operation also can be used with a mask to clear one or more bits. Each bit position in the mask that is set to 0 will force a 0 bit to appear in the result. The positions where the mask bit is set to 1 will take on the value of the source variable.

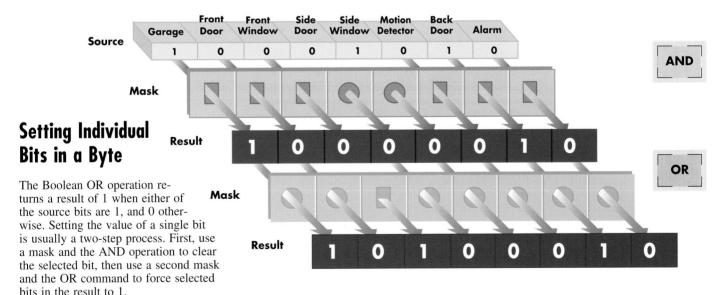

Setting Individual Bits in a Byte

The Boolean OR operation returns a result of 1 when either of the source bits are 1, and 0 otherwise. Setting the value of a single bit is usually a two-step process. First, use a mask and the AND operation to clear the selected bit, then use a second mask and the OR command to force selected bits in the result to 1.

Hexadecimal and Boolean operations are confusing to many beginning programmers. The good news is that you can do an enormous amount of programming without using hexadecimal at all, especially if you are using a high-level language such as BASIC.

Pointers

EVERY VARIABLE HAS a name, a value, and a location in memory. Some languages support a type of variable that has the ability to hold the location (or address) of another variable. This type of variable is called a *pointer*.

Pointers are often used when a portion of your program can perform a specific operation on a variable, but you need to perform that same operation on many different variables during the course of the program. You could make a copy of that program segment for each variable that needs to be worked on, but that is very wasteful. It is much more efficient to write the program segment in such a way that it can use a pointer to determine which variable to work on. That way, your program only needs to change the pointer variable to point to each of the variables you need, then use the same program segment for each one.

Some languages, such as C, require the programmer to explicitly define and use pointers to perform a task like the one just described. C gives you a choice between referring to a variable by name and letting the language look up the address, or using a pointer to give the language the address directly. Either way, you are able to find the contents of the variable. Other languages, such as some versions of BASIC, do not allow explicit use of pointers at all, but do allow you to use them implicitly under some conditions. Yet other languages, such as C++, give you a choice.

It Is Polite to Point!

A pointer contains the location of another variable. A pointer can be used to access the value of the variable to which it refers. This is called *indirect access*. When pointers are directed to other pointers, this is called *double indirection*.

Who Saved the Cat?

Parent: "I don't know, but that girl over there knows. Her name is Samantha— go ask her." (*double indirection*)

Variable Name	**Parent**
Type	Pointer to a pointer
Size	4 bytes
Contents	7000
Location	8000

In the C Language

```
typedef char *STRING;
// Define a C string type
STRING **Parent;
// Parent is a pointer to a pointer to a STRING
Parent = &Samantha;
// It contains the address of variable Samantha
```

The locations and variable sizes given here are for illustration purposes only and can vary, depending on the system you use.

Firefighter: "I did. My name is George."
(*direct access of variable*)

Samantha: "Over there—he saved
the cat. His name is George."
(*indirect access of variable*)

Variable Name	**FireFighter**
Type	String
Size	6 bytes
Contents	"George"
Location	6000

In the C Language

```
typedef char *STRING
// Define a C string type
STRING FireFighter = "George"
```

Variable Name	**Samantha**
Type	Pointer to a string
Size	4 bytes
Contents	6000
Location	7000

In the C Language

```
typedef char *STRING;
// Define a C string type
STRING *Samantha;
// Samantha is a pointer to a STRING
Samantha = &FireFighter;
// It contains the address of variable FireFighter
```

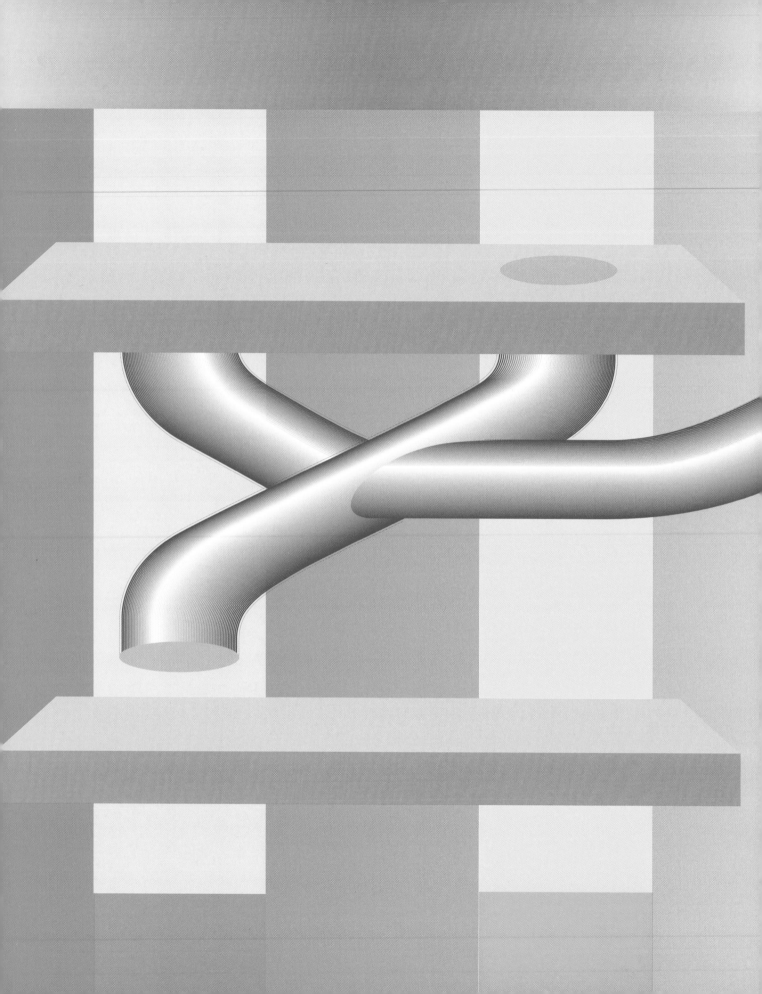

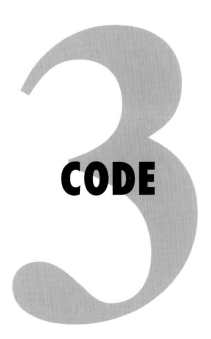

CODE

Chapter 8: Statements and Operators
52

Chapter 9: Blocks and Functions
58

Chapter 10: Program Flow
62

Chapter 11: Variable Declaration and Scoping
66

OVERVIEW

OW THAT YOU know how variables store data, it's time to take the next step and find out how to do something with those variables. In order to manipulate the data contained in variables, a computer needs a list of instructions to perform—a program. The instructions in a program are often called the program *code*. A computer *executes* code when it performs the instructions that the code describes.

There are hundreds of different computer languages, but most of them share certain fundamental operations. The exact way to specify a particular operation can vary dramatically from one language to the next, but once you understand how to perform an operation in one language, it usually is not difficult to find out how to perform it in another language.

Computer languages may use different commands, also known as *syntax*, to perform particular operations. However, once you know that the operation exists, it is only a matter of time before you learn how to perform it in a given language. It's somewhat like driving an unfamiliar car for the first time. It often takes a few minutes to find out where they hid the light switch for that car, but since you know that every car has headlights, you can be confident that sooner or later you will find the switch.

There are several fundamental types of instructions that are common in most computer languages. *Statements* are the simplest commands in a language, and are used primarily to copy data between variables or to perform calculations on variables.

Program blocks, *functions*, and *subroutines* are small groups of code that perform operations that you define. Programs can contain many thousands of lines of code. Computer languages allow you to break these lines into these smaller groups in order to make it easier for programmers to manage code. *Program flow* consists of the commands in a language that allow a program to make decisions based on calculated results. Program flow controls the sequence in which your program's instructions are executed.

Variable and memory management are critical because of the very large amounts of data that programs can access. Computer languages provide commands that allow you to organize variables into related groups that are easier to work with.

Statements and Operators

Assignment:
Only the variable on the left side of the assignment operation is changed. The right side of the assignment expression contains operators and *arguments*, variables or constant values such as numbers or strings (depending on the type of operator).

**Assignment
A = B**

5   7

BEFORE

=

7   7

AFTER

A   B

**Assignment
A = A + B + 8**

5   7   8

BEFORE

+

20   7

AFTER

A   B

( )

(x)   (x)
Parentheses
Expressions within parentheses are always calculated first.

BASIC only

∧

x^Y   **Exponentiation**   x^Y
The ∧ (caret) symbol is used in BASIC to perform the exponentiation operation. In C, the ∧ symbol is used for the Boolean XOR function.

–

-x   **Negation**   -x
The minus sign is used to indicate that a number is negative.

/ *

÷   **Division and Multiplication**   x
The / (fraction) symbol and * symbol are used in most languages instead of the ÷ and x that you may be used to. C uses the % symbol, and BASIC the MOD keyword to calculate the remainder after an integer division.

*

Boolean Comparison Operators
Both BASIC and C provide Boolean operations that operate on each bit in an argument. C also provides Boolean operations that work on the value of an argument in which any nonzero value is TRUE, and zero is FALSE. The || and && operators are the logical OR and AND operators.

Boolean Operators
C uses the |, ^, and & characters for the OR, XOR, and AND Boolean operations. BASIC uses the keywords OR, XOR, and AND.

Complement
C's ~ and BASIC's NOT operators invert the state of each bit in a variable. For example, ~01100011 results in 10011100. C's ! operator returns TRUE if the argument is FALSE, and FALSE if the argument is TRUE.

Precedence:
Statements can contain a complex series of operations. A language has rules of precedence that determine the order in which operations occur. Be careful—each language may have its own precedence rules! For example, in the equation $X = 3 + 2 * 5$, simple left-to-right precedence such as that used in the language APL leads to the result 25, whereas in C or BASIC the multiplication will occur first giving the result 13. The samples here describe the rules for C and for Visual Basic (which is representative of most versions of BASIC).

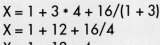

$$X = 1 + 3 * 4 + 16/(1 + 3)$$
$$X = 1 + 12 + 16/4$$
$$X = 1 + 12 + 4$$
$$X = 17$$

Equivalence
The equal and nonequal operators return a result of TRUE or FALSE. C uses the == and != for equal and nonequal. BASIC uses = and <> for these.

Comparison
The greater-than, greater-than-or-equal-to, less-than, and less-than-or-equal-to operators return a Boolean result of TRUE or FALSE.

Addition and Subtraction
The + operator in BASIC also is used to concatenate strings. For example, StringVar = "Hello " + "Goodbye" will set variable StringVar to "Hello Goodbye".

Shift
The C language uses the << and >> operators to shift the bits in an integer numeric argument to the right or left. In binary, 01001100 >> 1 results in 00100110.

Blocks and Functions

PROGRAMMING INVOLVES BREAKING a complex task that you wish the computer to perform into individual instructions, or code statements, that the computer can execute. This is something that we human beings do all the time. Consider the task of boiling a pot of water. You can break this task into the smaller tasks of finding a pot, taking it to a faucet, filling it with water, taking it to a stove, turning on the stove, placing the pot over the heat, and waiting until the water boils.

Boiling water is a relatively simple task—we broke it down into only seven steps. But even simple programs can have thousands of statements. Complex programs can run into millions of statements. One of the most important things a programmer needs to do is to manage the complexity of a program. No human being can entirely understand or remember all the statements in a one-million-statement program. It's much easier to understand how a program works—and to develop one—if you divide the program into blocks of code that have specific functions. This process is also essential to dividing up tasks in large projects that involve more than one programmer.

There are several ways to group statements. A block of code is simply a group of statements that performs a particular task; the statements that make up a block of code appear one after the other in a program. The programming language determines the way in which blocks are identified. The C language uses the { and } characters to bracket a block of code; Pascal uses the Begin and End statements; and BASIC uses several methods, depending on the type of block. Blocks of code can contain other blocks of code in an unending hierarchy.

A function, subroutine, or procedure is a block of code that has been assigned a name, just as a variable is a block of data that has a name. With variables, you use the name to reference data. With functions, you use the name of the block to reference and execute a block of code. This makes functions the most important way in which you can group statements. When you call a function or subroutine, the code in that function is executed, and execution continues from the statement after the function call. It is possible to provide a function with data on which it will operate. Variables called *parameters* accomplish this objective. It is also possible for a function to return data to the code that called it.

Some languages use the term *subroutine* or *procedure* to refer to a function that does not return any data.

Boiling Water—
From a Computer's Point of View

Marv is a fictional robot who, like most robots, is controlled by a computer. This computer is programmed in an imaginary language called "Marvish," which instructs Marv to perform certain operations. Marv has a single arm that can rotate and grab and release objects. He also has the ability to go over to a place or object and to wait a specified time. Here are the five commands that Marv knows:

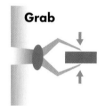
Grab

Release

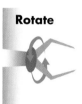
Rotate

MoveTo()

Wait()

Marv has a built-in function for boiling water. The function is called BoilWater() and works by calling four other functions: FindPot(), FillWithWater(), BringToStove(), and HeatWater(). Each of these functions is made up of statements in the Marvish language. Breaking a complex task into a hierarchy of functions is a very important part of programming. Broken down, here's what function BoilWater() might look like:

```
Function BoilWater()
      FindPot()
      FillWithWater()
      BringToStove()
      HeatWater()
End Function
Function FindPot()
      MoveTo(Pot)
      Grab
      MoveTo(Sink)
      Release
End Function
Function FillWithWater()
      MoveTo(Faucet)
      Grab
      Rotate
      Release
End Function
Function BringToStove()
      MoveTo(Pot)
      Grab
      MoveTo(Stove)
      Release
End Function
Function HeatWater()
      MoveTo(Heat)
      Grab
      Rotate
      Wait(15 minutes)
End Function
```

You may have noticed a couple of problems with this program. For one thing, Marv is not a good environmentalist—he never turns off the water at the end of the FillWithWater() function. He also doesn't turn off the stove once the water is boiling. You might also want to rearrange some of the commands. For example, one could argue that steps 3 and 4 of the FindPot() function should be parts of the FillWithWater() function instead of parts of the FindPot() function.

The process of fixing these problems is called *debugging* and will be discussed later.

Top-Level Function: BoilWater()
Second-Level Functions:

FindPot()

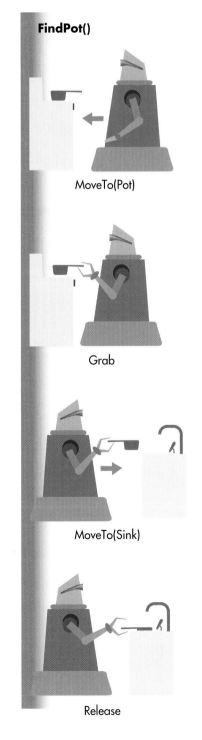

MoveTo(Pot)

Grab

MoveTo(Sink)

Release

FillWithWater()

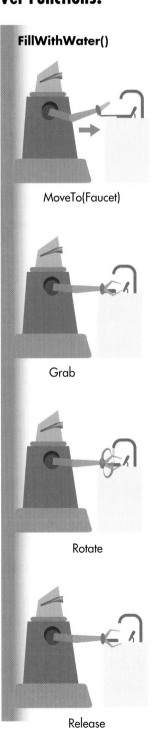

MoveTo(Faucet)

Grab

Rotate

Release

BringToStove()

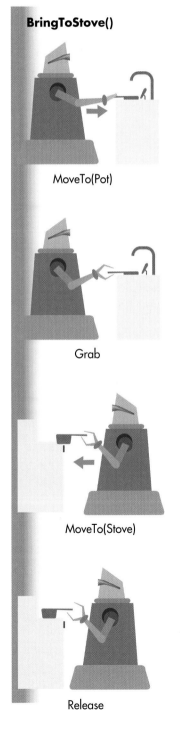

MoveTo(Pot)

Grab

MoveTo(Stove)

Release

HeatWater()

MoveTo(Heat)

Grab

Rotate

Wait(15 Minutes)

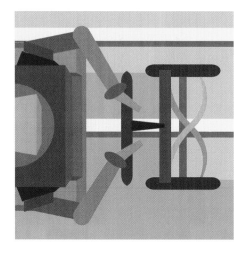

Program Flow

I F A PROGRAM were limited to performing a series of instructions one after the other, it would be very limited indeed. A computer's real power derives from using the data available to a program to choose which blocks of code to execute. As a programmer, you define the comparisons or rules that your program will use to decide which operations to perform.

There are several statements that computer languages use to control program flow. The *If...Then statement* executes a block of code that is specified after the word *Then* only if the comparison specified after the word *If* is found to be true. The *For statement* (also known as *For...Next* in BASIC) executes a block of code many times, each time changing the value of a *counter variable*—an integer variable used as a counter. The *While statement* executes a block of code as long as a specified comparison is found to be true. The *Select* or *Switch statement* is often used to select one of a group of blocks of code to execute, based on the value of a variable.

Some programmers actually draw a graphical description of the flow of a program, called a *flowchart*. This is especially useful for smaller code fragments, or for understanding the overall structure of a complex program. Many programmers prefer to use an English-like description of the operation of a program, called *pseudocode*. Pseudocode describes the operation of a program in general terms. The imaginary language "Marvish" used in the examples in the last chapter and in this one is, in fact, pseudocode.

Program Flow: Mowing the Lawn

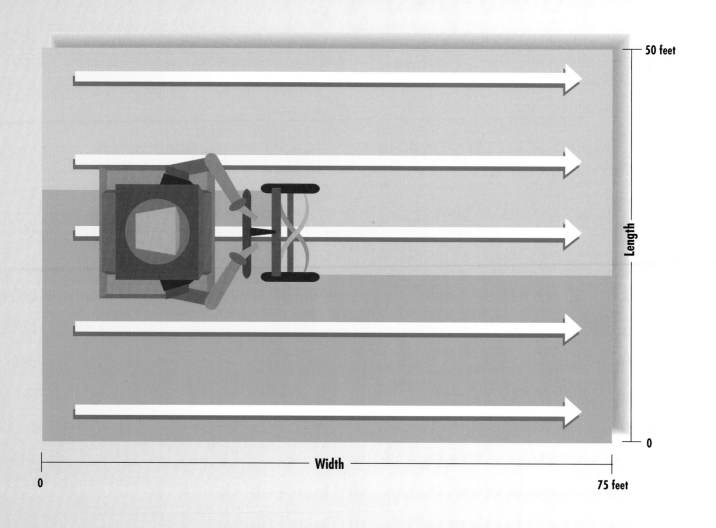

Our robot, Marv, has been retired from boiling water and has been reprogrammed to cut grass on a lawn that is 75 feet wide and 50 feet long. To perform his new task, Marv had to learn how to count and how to make decisions. His new function MowTheLawn() uses variables named *Length* and *Width* to determine where Marv is. The command Push tells Marv to push the lawnmower forward one foot. Marv also knows how to determine when he is stuck, and how to dislodge any obstacles in his path. A flowchart shows the sequence of operations for function MowTheLawn(). A rectangular box represents a statement. A diamond indicates a decision. In a decision, a comparison operation is performed and the result determines which statement the program will execute next.

Loops and Comparisons

To move Marv across the width of the lawn, the program must increment the variable Width from the value 0 through the value 75. The For statement can accomplish this. In order to cover the entire lawn, Marv must cross the width of the lawn many times, changing the *Length* variable each time. An If...Then statement is used at each position to determine if the lawnmower is stuck. The ' character is used to indicate a comment that is not part of the program itself. Note how indentation is often used to make the blocks of code easier to identify.

The program in Marvish might look something like this:

```
Function MowTheLawn()
    For Length = Ø to 5Ø
        ' Everything within this block (up to the Next Length
        ' command) will be repeated for each value of Length.
        For Width = Ø to 75
            ' Everything within this block will be repeated for
            ' each value of Width
            Push
            ' Stuck is a variable that is TRUE if the mower
            ' is stuck
            if(Stuck) then DislodgeObstacle()
            ' The Next statement marks the end of the block
            ' created by the preceding For statement, and
            ' increments the Width variable by 1.
        Next Width
    Next Length
End Function
```

The For statement increments a variable by a fixed amount each time the computer reaches the associated Next statement. The default increment is 1, but a real language will let you specify any value.

Purists will note that this particular program has Marv reaching the end of the row, then continuing at the start of the next row with no indication of how he got there. For this example, we can assume that Marv has been programmed to lift the mower and proceed automatically to wherever the *Width* and *Length* variables tell him he is supposed to be. In a real program, the width and length of the lawn would probably be stored in variables that could be used in the For statements so that Marv could cut any size lawn.

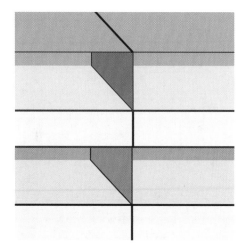

Variable Declaration and Scoping

EVERY PROGRAMMING LANGUAGE provides a mechanism for defining variables. This process is referred to as *declaring* or *dimensioning* variables. Declaring a variable causes the programming language to allocate space for the variable in memory, and allows you to specify the variable type.

You already have seen how you can use blocks and functions to manage the complexity of program code. The same problem of complexity exists when we deal with variables. A large program might require thousands of variables and it can be exceedingly difficult to keep track of them all by name.

Programming languages use several techniques to manage data. In Part 4, you will find out how variables can be grouped together into arrays and structures in much the same way functions group code statements. Another technique is based on the fact that, in many cases, variables are needed only for a brief time. For example, a function may need to use variables while performing a task. If these variables are used only by a single function, there is no reason for them to be accessible from outside that function. In fact, there is no reason to waste memory holding those variables when that function is not executing. Most languages provide one or more methods for creating private or *temporary variables.*

The rules that determine which variables are accessible by what code are called the *scoping rules* for a language, since they determine the scope of a variable. The most common scopes of variables are global, static, and dynamic variables, as well as parameters.

Global variables typically are declared when a program first starts running. They exist throughout the life of the program, and are accessible by any function in the program.

Static variables also exist throughout the life of a program, but usually are accessible only by a single function or the functions in just a portion of your program.

Dynamic variables are temporary variables that exist only while a particular function or block of code is executing. Once that block of code stops executing, these variables no longer exist and the memory that was allocated to hold them is released.

A *parameter* is a special kind of variable that is used to pass information to a function. *Function parameters* are dynamic variables—they exist only for the function in which they are called. Parameters can be passed *by reference* or *by value*. When a parameter is passed by reference, the parameter variable in the function refers to the same location in memory as does the original variable that appears in the function call. This means that changing the parameter also changes the original variable. When a parameter is passed by value, the function makes a temporary copy of the data in the original variable. Changing the parameter in this situation has *no* effect on the original variable. Each language has its own syntax for determining whether a parameter is passed by reference or by value.

Variable Declaration and Scope

Variables have two characteristics: lifetime and visibility. The *lifetime* of a variable determines when and for how long it exists. The visibility determines what parts of the program can access that variable. Imagine if we were to create a computer program that simulated the operation of the Federal and State governments. We could start by defining some variables that contain information on each senator.

1 We've allocated two variables for U.S. Senator Grey and two for U.S. Senator Smith—one for each representing hair length, the other representing their vote. Since the U.S. Senate is the highest level of government, senators represent people on the state and local level as well. The variables used for these senators are therefore global variables that are visible to all functions in the program, and they exist as long as the program is running.

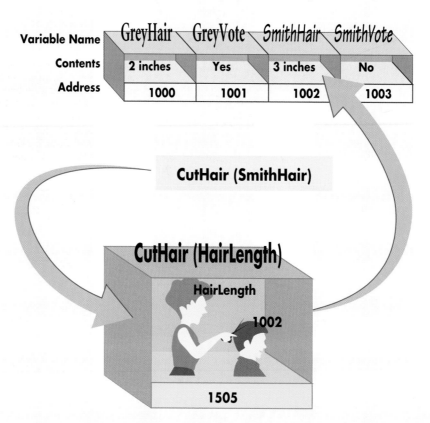

Variable Name	GreyHair	GreyVote	SmithHair	SmithVote
Contents	2 inches	Yes	3 inches	No
Address	1000	1001	1002	1003

CutHair (SmithHair)

CutHair (HairLength)

HairLength

1002

1505

3 The senate barbershop can serve any senator—U.S. or state. The barbershop might be represented by the function CutHair(HairLength), where HairLength is a parameter to the function indicating the current length of a senator's hair. Calling the function creates a new temporary variable called *HairLength* whose lifetime and visibility is limited to the barbershop function. In order to allow function CutHair to change the value of the calling variable, the parameter is passed *by reference*. In this example, the HairLength parameter actually contains the location in memory of the calling variable *SmithHair*. Changing the value of parameter HairLength thus actually changes the contents of *SmithHair*.

2 This state senate has variables for two *other* senators: Senator Smith and Senator Fox. When you are in the statehouse (or the function describing the statehouse), any reference to Senator Smith's variables will refer to the state senator—*not* the U.S. senator by the same name. These variables exist as long as the program, but the visibility is limited. State senator variables are visible only within the statehouse function.

The presence of variables *SmithHair* and *SmithVote* serves to hide the visibility of the global variables of the same name.

Variable Name	SmithHair	SmithVote	FoxHair	FoxVote
Contents	8 inches	Yes	3 inches	Yes
Address	1300	1301	1302	1303

TallyVote (FoxVote)

TallyVote (ThisVote)

ThisVote

no
Yes

yes
yes
yes
no
yes
no
no

1405

4 The vote-tallying function is called for each senator and is represented by the function

```
Function TallyVote(ThisVote)
```

ThisVote is also a temporary variable whose lifetime and visibility is limited to this function. Since there is no need for the function to change the value of the senator's actual vote, the parameter is passed *by value*. *ThisVote* actually contains a copy of the calling variable; thus, in this example, changing the value of variable *ThisVote* within the function will have no effect on variable *FoxVote*.

5 A function can create additional temporary variables that exist only within the scope of that function. A vote-report function might look like this in pseudocode:

```
Integer Function CountNoVotes()
    Dim SenatorNumber As Integer    ' Temporary senator counter variable
    Dim NoVotes As Integer          ' Temporary vote-counter variable
    NoVotes = 0
    YesVotes = 0
    For SenatorNumber = 1 to 100
        If Senator(SenatorNumber) voted No then
            NoVotes = NoVotes + 1 ' Increment the value of NoVotes
        Else YesVotes = YesVotes + 1
        Endif
    Next SenatorNumber
    return(NoVotes)
End Function
```

Declaring Variables

Every language has its own way of declaring variables. Declaring a variable causes the language to allocate space for the variable in memory and lets you define a name for that variable. It also specifies the variable type so that the language can detect mistakes such as attempting to add a string to an integer. Here are some sample variable declarations.

In BASIC	Dim ACounter As Integer Dim AString As String
In C	int ACounter; char *APointerToAString;

ORGANIZING DATA

CONTENTS

Chapter 12: Arrays
76

Chapter 13: Structures
82

Chapter 14: Stacks and Queues
88

Chapter 15: Linked Lists
94

Chapter 16: Decision Trees
100

OVERVIEW

VARIABLES AND CODE are the building blocks of any computer language. The first step in assembling those building blocks into a working program is for you to decide how to organize your data.

You could place each item of data into its own variable. This approach works well with very small programs, but what about programs that contain thousands or hundreds of thousands of data items? No human could keep track of that many individual variables.

Most modern languages provide several techniques for organizing data so that you can manage even complex information. The two most important of these techniques, arrays and structures, allow you to create variables that are aggregates, or combinations, of the simple variable types that were covered earlier in this book.

An *array* allows you to create a variable that contains a sequence of data items of a given type, each identified by an index into the array. For example, a classroom teacher could use an array to list all the students in a class. Each item in the array would contain the name of one of the students in the class.

A *structure* allows you to create a new type of variable. This new variable is built from one or more other variables, arrays, or structures that contain related information. For example, a teacher could create a structure containing information about a student. The structure might include the student's name, age, nickname, height, parents' names, and so on. It is possible for a structure to contain another structure or array.

Arrays and structures are built into most languages. There are a number of other techniques for organizing data that are not usually part of a language, but can be implemented very easily by a programmer. The most common of these are stacks, queues, linked lists, and trees. These techniques allow you to place large amounts of data into lists that your program organizes.

The importance of choosing a good organization for your data cannot be overstated. Most people think the best way to improve the performance of a program is to use a faster computer. The truth is, designing an efficient program from the start optimizes its performance. The right data organization can save you hours of work and dramatically improve the execution speed of your program. Many programmers consider choice of data structures and data organization to be the first step in the design of any program.

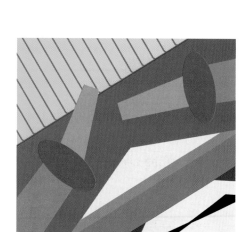

Arrays

TAKE A CARD, any card. Card games such as blackjack frequently are the first type of program that a beginning programmer writes. They are good learning exercises, as they frequently demand skills beyond those used in other types of programs.

You must begin by deciding how to represent a deck of cards in your program. You could create 52 string variables named *card1*, *card2*, *card3*, and so forth, then load each variable with a description such as "ace of clubs," "two of diamonds," and so on. There are several problems with this approach. First, you would have to deal with 52 different variables. Second, there would be no good way to manipulate these variables under program control—and you would need to create code to handle each one of the variables when performing tasks such as shuffling and dealing from the deck.

A better approach is to create an array variable called *Deck* that contains 52 entries. Each item in the array has an index ranging from 1 to 52. This approach will solve both of the problems described above. First, you will have only one variable instead of 52. Next, since you can use another variable to specify the index, it will be easy to access any entry under program control. Variables in an array are accessed by referring to the name of the array followed by the index in parentheses or brackets, depending on the language. For example, the BASIC code to print the value of the card at the position specified by numeric variable N would be

```
Print Deck(N)
```

While you can use strings to describe cards, a more efficient approach might be to use integers to describe the cards. By assigning each card a number from 1 to 52, you can use simple calculations to determine the suit and rank (number) for each card. For example, if cards 1 through 13 are the ace through king of clubs, 14 through 26 are diamonds, 27 through 39 are hearts, and 40 through 52 are spades, you can divide (card value − 1) by 13 to determine the suit and use the remainder to determine the card's rank. This can greatly simplify a program such as one that plays blackjack, in which you frequently need to add the ranks of the cards in a hand to make sure that they do not exceed 21, or a poker program where you must match ranks and suits to determine the strength of a hand.

It's in the Cards

1 Arrays often are an ideal way to represent a group of data items that are all of the same type. The computer can access individual items in an array very efficiently—calculating the address of an item is usually a simple multiplication and addition operation.

A deck of cards can be represented by an array with 52 integers. You can initialize and shuffle a deck using the following BASIC code:

```basic
Din Deck(52) As Integer

Sub shuffle ()
    Dim index As Integer
    Dim cardholder As Integer    ' Temporary variable for holding a card
    Dim swapcard As Integer      ' Location for swap during shuffling
    ' Initialize each entry to a unique value
    For index = 1 To 52
        Deck(index) = index
    Next index
    ' Now shuffle by randomizing the order of the cards
    For index = 1 To 52
        ' The Rnd function returns a random number from Ø to 1
        ' The Int function returns the integer part of a number
        swapcard = Int(Rnd * 52) + 1 ' Choose a random location
        ' Swap the card at location index with that at location swapcard
        cardholder = Deck(index)
        Deck(index) = Deck(swapcard)
        Deck(swapcard) = cardholder
    Next index
End Sub
```

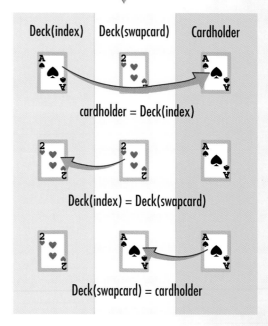

Deck(index)   Deck(swapcard)   Cardholder

cardholder = Deck(index)

Deck(index) = Deck(swapcard)

Deck(swapcard) = cardholder

NOTE Have you ever wondered why programmers often use games as examples? A quick look at any of the advanced simulator games available today proves a curious point—the competitive nature of the leisure software market forces game technology to be at the leading edge of software technology in general.

2 Two simple functions can be used to determine the suit and the rank of each card in the deck:

```
Function SuitOfCard (cardnum As Integer)
    ' Given a card number, return the suit as a number 1-4
    SuitOfCard = Int((cardnum - 1) / 13) + 1
End Function

Function RankOfCard (cardnum As Integer)
    ' Given a card number, return the rank as a number 1 - 13
    RankOfCard = Int((cardnum - 1) Mod 13) + 1
End Function
```

Dealing from the Deck array of cards into the hands represented by the Hand array can be accomplished using For…Next loops as follows:

```
Sub Deal ()
    Dim TopCard As Integer
    Dim DealHand As Integer
    Dim CardInHand As Integer

    TopCard = 1 ' Start with the top card in the deck
    ' Loop through each hand
    For DealHand = 1 To 4
        ' Loop through each card in the hand
        For CardInHand = 1 To 5
            Hand(DealHand, CardInHand) = Deck(TopCard)
            ' Set TopCard to refer to the next card in the deck
            TopCard = TopCard + 1
        Next CardInHand
    Next DealHand
End Sub
```

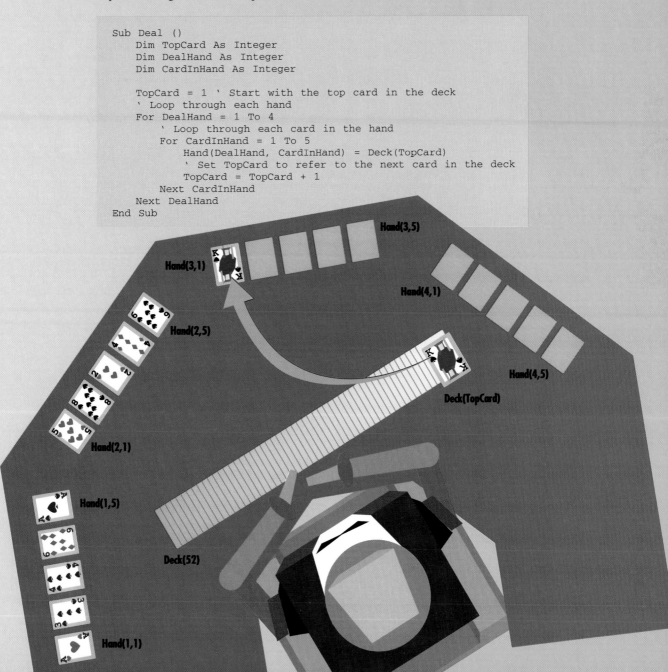

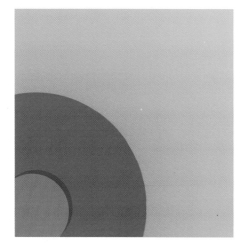

CHAPTER 13

Structures

CONSIDER WHAT HAPPENS when you want to call a friend on the telephone. Like most people, you probably have an address book that contains your friends' addresses and phone numbers. It might also list where they work, names of spouses and children, and perhaps even their birthdays. To find any of this information, all you need to do is look up your friend by name.

Why don't you keep different books for each piece of information? Why not a separate book for addresses, one for phone numbers, one for birthdays, and so on? The reason is clear: Arranging all the information in one place allows you to find everything you want to know about your friend with one search. It makes it easy to make corrections—if your friend moves, you need change only a single page in one book, instead of an address page in one book, a phone number in another, and so on.

Just as you arrange your phone book to keep related information in one place, computer languages make it possible to keep related data together. One of the best ways to accomplish this is by using a type of variable called a structure. Structures are also referred to in some languages as *user-defined variables*, *classes*, or *objects*. A *structure* is formed by combining other variables and structures.

Consider a program that is designed to keep track of a compact-disc collection. Each CD has a name, category, recording company, and artist. It also has a list of songs, each of which has a name and length. Since all these pieces of information relate closely to a compact disc, it makes sense to define a new type of variable that will represent a single CD. This new variable will contain other variables for the name, category, and other information, and also can contain an array of structures that hold information about a particular song. A compact disk collection could be represented by an array of these CD structures.

Using a structure in this manner has many advantages. It makes the program easier to understand, since the CD structure corresponds closely to the way a compact disc is organized in real life. It also simplifies the program by limiting the number of variables you need to deal with. It helps make the program more efficient by keeping related data close together—once your program has found a particular CD structure, it can quickly access any of the information in that structure.

Most languages allow you to access individual variables, or fields, of a structure using a period between the variable name and the field name. For example, if you have defined a structure called CD that contains a variable named *AlbumName* and created a variable of type CD called *Album1*, the name of the compact disc could be referenced using *Album1.AlbumName*.

Structures are becoming increasingly important to programmers as languages begin to incorporate new object-oriented technology. *Object-oriented* programming focuses on the creation and manipulation of structures and will be discussed in greater detail in Part 7.

Building Structures

1 Our old friend, Marv the robot, is working today as an electronic juke box, selecting from among a vast array of compact discs. His memory contains a list of all the available CDs, organized as an array of structures of a type called CD.

2 The CD structure, shown here defined in the BASIC language, contains information relating to each compact disc. It also contains an array of structures of a type called SongInfo that holds the name and length of each song. The SongInfo structure could be defined as follows:

```
Type SongInfo
       Name As String     ' The name
       Length As Integer  ' The length in seconds
End Type
```

```
Type CD
    Category as String
    Publisher as String
    Name as String
    Length as Long
    Artist as String
    Songs(15) as SONGINFO
        Songs(1)
        Songs(2)
        Songs(3)
        Songs(4)
        Songs(5)
        Songs(6)
        Songs(7)
        Songs(8)
        Songs(9)
        Songs(10)
        Songs(11)
        Songs(12)
        Songs(13)
        Songs(14)
        Songs(15)
End Type
```

Electronic Music	
Robotic Records	
Sing Along with Marv	
2100 ' seconds	
Marv the Robot	
Like a Robot	**194**
Not the Tin Woodsman	**104**
Clank Clang	**201**
Heart of Steel	**189**

3 The C language also provides extensive support for structures. The CD structure in C might be defined as follows:

```
struct SongInfo {
    char *Name;
    int Length;
};

struct CD {
    char *Category;
    char *Publisher;
    char *Name;
    long Length;
    char *Artist;
    struct SongInfo Songs[15];
};
```

Stacks and Queues

"**P**LEASE TAKE OUT the trash," requests another member of your household. You put down the book you are reading and carefully mark the page. As you walk to the door with the garbage bag in hand, you are interrupted by the ringing of the telephone. You put down the trash bag, noting where you left it, and proceed to answer the phone. When you are finished talking, you go to where you remember placing the trash bag and take it out. When you return, you sit down, open the book to where you were, and continue with your reading.

Computer programs frequently need to stop what they are doing in order to handle another task. In fact, every time you call a function, you are telling your program to stop executing the current function and branch to a new function. Just as you need to remember what you are doing when interrupted, so a computer program must carefully record where it is in a function and the values of variables that belong to that function before it branches to the next function. Programs do this by storing information on a data structure called a stack. A *stack* is a list of data that works on *a last in first out* (LIFO) manner. The data most recently pushed onto the stack is the first data to be popped from the stack when the interrupting task is complete. It's somewhat like a stack of dishes in a kitchen, where the dish put away last sits on the top of the stack and is the first one used next time you eat.

Most programming languages use a built-in stack to handle function calls. This process is transparent to programmers unless there are so many function calls that the amount of data stored on the stack exceeds the amount of memory available to the stack, which can cause a stack overflow error. Programmers can also create their own stacks any time they need to save the state of a program in order to perform a different task and then restore the program to its previous state.

Queues are similar to stacks except that they operate in a *first in, first out* (FIFO) manner. A *queue* is like a line where information can be stored until needed. Think of a line at an amusement park, where people start at the end and leave the front in the same order in which they arrived. Queues are frequently used to store incoming data from a serial port until the program is ready to use it.

From a programmer's point of view, stacks and queues are usually created out of arrays or linked lists (a type of data organization that will be discussed in Chapter 15). The code involved in implementing stacks and queues is quite simple, and is a good project for beginning programmers.

Building Structures

Stacks are used when you need to save the state of a program for later reference—especially when you might need to save more than one state. Placing data on the stack is called *pushing* data onto the stack; removing data is called *popping* data from the stack. This is what the stack might look like for a program that simulates the scenario described at the beginning of the chapter.

PUSH

Answering phone

You can remove data only from the top of the stack, but it is still possible for a program to access information that is farther down. Programs use stacks to store variables that are local to functions. Each time you call a function, variables for that function are pushed onto the stack along with the information needed to return to the calling function when the current function call is complete. Those variables belong to that particular function call. If you call the same function again, that function call will have its own set of local variables that may have their own values. This makes it possible for functions to be *reentrant*, meaning they can call themselves. A function that calls itself uses an important programming technique called *recursion* which will be discussed in Chapter 18.

Bag is by door

Taking out trash

Page 156

Reading a book

BOS   TOS   EOS

A stack can be implemented in an array in BASIC by creating two functions, Push and Pop, as follows:

```
Dim Stack(3Ø) As Integer    ' An array containing the stack
Dim BOS As Integer  ' Beginning of stack
Dim EOS As Integer   ' End of stack
Dim TOS As Integer   ' Current top of stack

BOS = 1       ' First entry in stack
EOS = 3Ø      ' End of stack
TOS = 1       ' Initial top of stack

Sub Push (value As Integer)
    If TOS > EOS Then Exit Sub  ' Stack is full
    ' Place data in stack
    Stack(TOS) = value
    TOS = TOS + 1' Increment the top of stack pointer
End Sub

Function Pop () As Integer
    ' Nothing to return if stack is empty
    If TOS = BOS Then Exit Function
    TOS = TOS - 1        ' Point to top data item
    Pop = Stack(TOS)        ' Return the top of stack
End Function
```

A real application would include error-reporting code to notify the application when an attempt was made to push data onto a full stack, or pop data from an empty stack.

Answering phone

Bag is by door

Taking out trash

Page 156

Reading a book

Waiting in Line

Queues are used to handle data in the order in which it arrives. It's just like waiting in line at an amusement park—first come, first served.

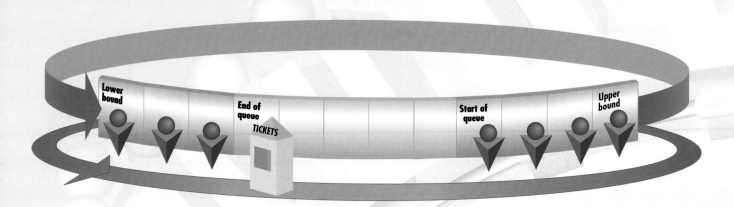

A queue can be implemented in an array, but unlike in a stack, the start and end of the queue both move. In the amusement park line, each time a person leaves the front of the queue, everyone moves forward. In software, a queue is typically implemented in an array. Moving all of the entries in the array each time data is removed from the queue would be horribly inefficient. Instead of moving the data, we use pointer variables to refer to the start and end of the queue and change them instead. It is therefore necessary to handle the case where the end of the queue reaches the last location in the array. We do this in the program by "wrapping" the pointers to the start of the array whenever the end of the array is reached. Two BASIC functions, AddToQueue and RemoveFromQueue, demonstrate this.

```
Dim Queue(3Ø) As Integer      ' An array containing the queue
Dim LowerBound As Integer     ' Beginning of array
Dim UpperBound As Integer     ' End of array
Dim EndOfQueue As Integer     ' End of queue (next free spot)
Dim StartOfQueue As Integer   ' Start of queue

LowerBound = 1
UpperBound = 3Ø
EndOfQueue = 1
StartOfQueue = 1       ' Queue starts empty
```

```
Sub AddToQueue (Value As Integer)
     Dim NewStart As Integer
     ' Place value before current start position
     NewStart = StartOfQueue - 1
     ' Wrap to end of array
     If NewStart < LowerBound Then NewStart = UpperBound
     If NewStart = EndOfQueue Then Exit Sub ' Queue is full
     Queue(NewStart) = Value
     StartOfQueue = NewStart ' New value for start
End Sub

Function RemoveFromQueue () As Integer
     ' Start = End is defined as an empty queue
     If StartOfQueue = EndOfQueue Then Exit Function
     EndOfQueue = EndOfQueue - 1
     ' Wrap around to end of array
     If EndOfQueue < LowerBound Then EndOfQueue = UpperBound
     RemoveFromQueue = Queue(EndOfQueue)
End Function
```

This particular example shows data being added to the left of the queue and removed from the right in much the same way people join and leave the amusement park ride shown above. It would be equally possible to reverse the direction and add data on the right and remove it from the left. You would need to modify the code so that the queue positions increment instead of decrement, and wrap around from the end of the array to the beginning. There is no need to prefer one direction over the other—both methods work equally well.

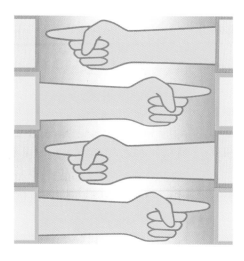

Linked Lists

YOU'VE ALREADY SEEN how arrays can dramatically improve the organization and efficiency of your programs. But as powerful as they are, arrays have their limitations. For one thing, inserting data into an array can be a very slow process—you must move all the entries from the insertion position to the end of the array in order to make room for the new entry. The same applies to the process of deleting entries if you wish to avoid unused "holes" in the array. The size of the array is another concern. Most languages do not allow you to change the size of an array once it has been declared. This means that you must allocate enough space for the largest array you think you will need. Space you allocate that is not needed goes to waste.

The solution to these problems lies in the concept of *indirection*—the idea that one variable can act as a pointer to another variable. (You saw this principle at work in Chapter 7.) You can create a linked list, which consists of a group of structures in which each structure contains a pointer variable that refers to the next structure in the list. The final structure in the list has its pointer variable set to a special value (typically, zero or NULL) to indicate that it is at the end of the list.

Inserting data into linked lists and deleting data from them is extremely fast—all you need to do is adjust a couple of pointer variables. There is no need to add variables to a linked list until they are actually needed. Linked lists are used in many common programming tasks. Spreadsheets use linked lists for storage—only cells that contain data take up space in memory. Operating systems use linked lists to keep track of the free space in disk and in memory. This is essential, since space is constantly being allocated and deallocated.

Linked lists perform better than arrays when it comes to inserting and deleting items in a list, and managing memory use, but they have disadvantages as well. For example, finding a particular entry in a linked list requires scanning through all the preceding entries, whereas finding an entry in an array frequently requires just a simple address calculation based on the index and size of the array variables. Linked lists also have slightly greater overhead in terms of memory use, since each entry must have a pointer variable. Simple linked lists can be scanned only in one direction, though it is common to create double linked lists in which each entry has a second pointer variable that points backward to the preceding entry in the list.

What about languages that don't support pointers? In those languages, it is still possible to implement linked lists using arrays. You simply create an array that will hold a pool of available entries for use in the list. Each entry contains a structure that has an integer variable that holds the index of the next entry in the list.

It is also possible for a structure to be part of an array and a linked list at the same time. This can be a powerful technique. For example, let's say you had an array of structures describing compact disks that you wanted to sort by the CD's name. You could sort them by changing their positions in the array, but this would involve moving a lot of data in memory. It would be much easier to add a new pointer variable to the structure and link the structures together. Instead of changing the order of the structures in the array, you could change their order in the linked list. This would be a simple matter of swapping a few pointers. You could add another pointer variable to the structure to create a second linked list that sorts the CDs by the artist's name as well. You can use multiple linked lists to organize data in as many different orders as you wish and never actually move the data in memory.

Linking Structures into Lists

You can add a pointer variable to a structure in order to create a linked list. The pointer can be a memory address in a language such as C that supports pointer types. It can also be a location in an array. In either case, a special value should be assigned to indicate that a pointer marks the end of the list. One of the advantages of linked lists over arrays is that they make it very efficient to insert and delete items in the list—pointer values are changed but no data is actually moved in memory. Functions in C for inserting and deleting items illustrate the process.

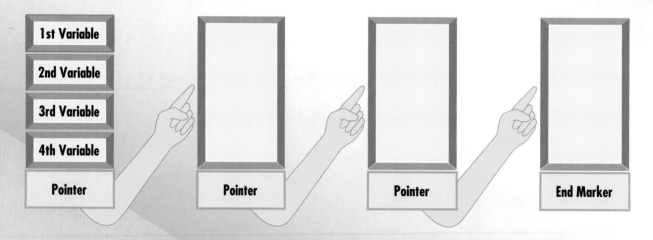

3 Function Remove() demonstrates how you might remove Entry2 from a linked list with three entries.

```
void Remove()
{
    // Set the list to the initial state shown.
    Entry1.ListPointer = &Entry2;
    Entry2.ListPointer = &Entry3;
    Entry3.ListPointer = Ø;


    // Now unlink Entry2
    Entry1.ListPointer = Entry2.ListPointer;


    // And clear the pointer in Entry2
    Entry2.ListPointer = Ø;
}
```

1 ListEntry is the name of a structure that can be used in a linked list. It contains a pointer variable that is used to create the link.

```
Struct ListEntry {
    int var1;    // Miscellaneous variables
    int var2;
    int var3;
    // Pointer is a pointer to ListEntry variables
    struct ListEntry *ListPointer;
};

// Define three ListEntry variables to work with
struct ListEntry Entry1, Entry2, Entry3;
```

2 Function Insert() demonstrates how you might add an item into a linked list. In this case Entry3 is added between Entry1 and Entry2.

```
// The word "void" in C indicates that a function
// does not return a value.
void Insert()
{
    // The & character means "take the address of..."
    // Thus &Entry2 means the location of
    //    variable Entry2 in memory.
    Entry1.ListPointer = &Entry2;



    // Now set Entry3 to point to Entry2
    Entry3.ListPointer = Entry1.ListPointer;




    // Now set Entry1 to point to Entry3
    Entry1.ListPointer = &Entry3;
}
```

Double Linked Lists

There is one problem with linked lists as shown. It is possible to scan the list in only one direction. For applications where you wish to traverse the list in both directions, a double linked list is appropriate. In this type of list, a second pointer variable is added to the structure, pointing to the previous entry in the list.

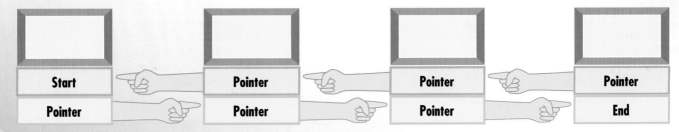

Decision Trees

HAVE YOU EVER drawn a diagram of your family tree? You start at the top with some distant ancestors. Below them are some children. They get married and have other children branching out below them, and so on…. Computer programs frequently use trees to represent this kind of branching. A genealogy program would obviously need a way to represent a family tree. The program could move a pointer down the tree to count descendants or to determine relationships. A chess program might use a *decision tree*—a tree where each branch tells the computer how to respond to an opponent's move. Trees are implemented using techniques similar to those used for linked lists. Instead of structures containing pointers to the next entry in a list, structures in trees contain two or more pointers to the branches, or *children*, for the entry. A tree can be designed to have as many children for each entry as you wish, but programmers frequently use a limited tree structure in which each entry can have only two children. This is called a *binary tree*. Each branch in a binary tree represents a decision; your program uses a rule to decide if the selected information is on the right or left branch.

One of the most common applications for binary trees is overcoming one of the major limitations of both arrays and linked lists: very slow searches. Searching for data in a linked list or array requires that you check every entry until you find the one for which you are looking. A binary search tree is set up so that for every entry in the tree, the values of its left child and any of its descendants are smaller than the values of its right child and any of its descendants. As you will see, finding a particular entry in such a tree is extremely fast. At each branch point in the tree you perform a simple comparison to decide whether the desired entry is down the left path or the right path. You can also insert and delete entries quickly using this method.

Binary search trees are not limited to numeric data. The value used for each entry can be a string, date, or any other data type. In fact, you can use any rule that defines a choice between the left and right branches of the tree.

Binary Trees

1 A binary tree has two branches for each variable, or *node*—in other words, each variable is a structure that has, at a minimum, a value and two pointers. The pointers point to left and right child variables.

Here you see a binary search tree where the values of the nodes range from 1 to 100. An *X* value indicates a "missing" node—one that does not actually exist in the tree.

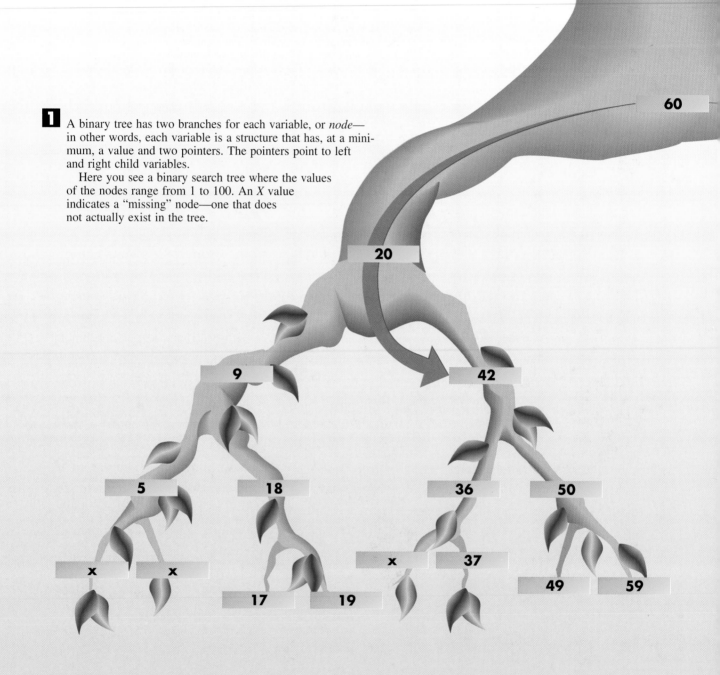

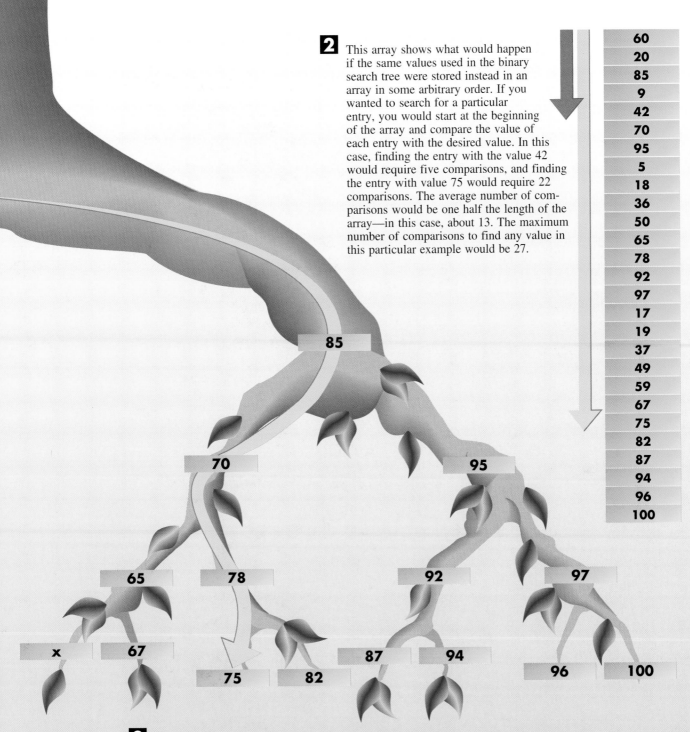

2 This array shows what would happen if the same values used in the binary search tree were stored instead in an array in some arbitrary order. If you wanted to search for a particular entry, you would start at the beginning of the array and compare the value of each entry with the desired value. In this case, finding the entry with the value 42 would require five comparisons, and finding the entry with value 75 would require 22 comparisons. The average number of comparisons would be one half the length of the array—in this case, about 13. The maximum number of comparisons to find any value in this particular example would be 27.

2 A search of a binary tree starts at the root. The node value is compared with the desired value. If the desired value is smaller, you proceed to the left child; if it is larger, you proceed to the right node. In this case, the entry with the value 42 is found after only three comparisons, and the entry with value 75 is found after only five comparisons. In fact, five comparisons is the maximum for any node in this particular tree.

For any full binary tree, the average number of comparisons will correspond roughly to the base 2 logarithm of the number of entries—a dramatic improvement over arrays in average search time, especially for very large amounts of data.

ALGORITHMS

CONTENTS

Chapter 17: Searching and Scanning
108

Chapter 18: Recursion
114

Chapter 19: Sorting
120

Chapter 20: Working with Files
126

Chapter 21: Graphics
132

Chapter 22: Simulations
140

OVERVIEW

TAKE SOME FLOUR and water, mozzarella cheese and tomato sauce. Add perhaps a pinch of oregano and garlic. Next, grab a roller and a pan or skillet and place them conveniently near your oven. What do you have?

Nothing. Just an interesting pile of utensils and ingredients. However, this particular collection of objects could be used to create a pizza—if you know how to put the elements together in a certain way. You could just start randomly combining the ingredients and experimenting with the tools, but it is much easier to grab a cookbook and read how to make pizza. A good pizza cookbook would not just tell you how to create one pizza, though. It would also have dozens of examples, and it would teach you enough about making pizza in general so that you could start with the basic ingredients and experiment, developing your own pizzas to suit your own tastes.

A computer language provides you with commands, the utensils of a program. The data structures that you define are the ingredients. But when it comes to figuring out how to put them together, a programmer uses an algorithm—a sort of cookbook of computer science.

An algorithm describes a way to perform a particular programming task. Each individual might actually implement the algorithm in a different way, just as each chef might use his or her knowledge to create a unique pizza. In fact, you could describe "Making a Pizza" as the name of an algorithm that could be used to create an infinite number of unique pizzas.

Algorithms are extremely valuable to programmers, because there are certain programming tasks that appear frequently in many different types of programs. Using a known algorithm to accomplish such a task eliminates the need for experimenting and figuring out how to solve the problem on your own. For example, if you have a list of data that you need to sort, you can simply read about sorting algorithms and choose one that is known to work well with the type of list you are using.

There are thousands, if not millions, of algorithms in existence. Most programmers spend a lot of time creating new ones, refining old ones, and trying to figure out which algorithms are best for particular tasks. The following chapters describe some of the most common algorithms and will provide a good start for you in developing your own "cookbook" for programming.

And just as a good pizza cookbook can provide you with the knowledge necessary to create an infinite variety of pizzas, your programming cookbook can open the door to the infinite number of possibilities that a computer language can provide.

Searching, Scanning, and Picket Fences

A picket fence can be described by two arrays. Each array has five entries representing the five fence posts. The first array, Heights, describes the height of each fence post. The second array, Locations, describes the distance of each fence post from the first one. For this example, the arrays are *one-based*—their indexes range from one to five.

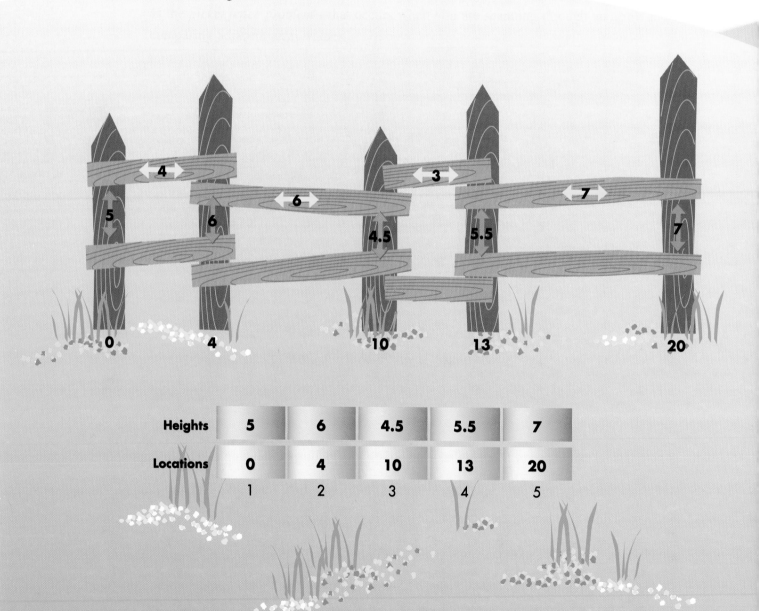

Heights	5	6	4.5	5.5	7
Locations	0	4	10	13	20
	1	2	3	4	5

Searching for a Fence Post

A simple array search checks each location in the array by using a For...Next loop, as shown in this example. Function FindHeight() returns the height of a fence post at a particular location, and returns 0 if there is no fence post at the position specified.

```
Function FindHeight (Position As Double) As Double
    Dim index As Integer
    For index = 1 To 5
        If Locations(index) = Position Then
            ' We found a post at the specified position
            ' So return the height at that position
            FindHeight = Heights(index)
            Exit Function    ' And exit the function
        End If
    Next index

    ' We didnít find a post at the location specified
    FindHeight = 0 ' Return 0 to indicate failure
End Function
```

Finding the Highest Fence Post

Function FindHighest() not only demonstrates a scanning algorithm, but also a common algorithm for finding a maximum value. The function starts by assuming that the first post is the highest, then scans through the rest to see if any are higher.

```
Function FindHighest () As Double
    Dim index As Integer
    ' Use this to hold the value of the current highest
    Dim CurrentHighest As Integer

    CurrentHighest = 1    ' First is highest so far
    For index = 2 To 5  ' Scan through the rest
        If Heights(index) > Heights(CurrentHighest) Then
            ' This is the highest found so far
            CurrentHighest = index
        End If
    Next index

    ' Now return the height at the highest location
    FindHighest = Heights(CurrentHighest)

End Function
```

Finding the Smallest Distance between Fence Posts

Function FindSmallestDistance() calculates the distance between every two fence posts and searches for the smallest distance. Even though there are five fence posts, there are only four spans between fence posts, thus we check only indexes 1 through 4.

```
Function FindSmallestDistance() As Integer
    Dim index As Integer
    Dim Distance As Integer
    Dim SmallestSoFar As Integer    ' Smallest distance so far

    SmallestSoFar = 32767    ' Largest possible integer

    For index = 1 To 4  ' Note we stop before the end
        ' Find the distance between this post and next
        Distance = Locations(index + 1) - Locations(index)
        If Distance < SmallestSoFar Then
            ' We found a smaller distance, so save it
            SmallestSoFar = Distance
        End If
    Next index

    FindSmallestDistance = SmallestSoFar

End Function
```

Variations on a Theme

Function FindSmallestDistance() is only one of many implementations of an algorithm that finds the smallest distance. For example, we could have varied the index from 2 to 5 instead of 1 to 4, and checked the location at (index − 1) instead of (index − 1). We could have stored the index that marks the start of the smallest span, instead of storing the span value itself. We could have scanned backward. We could have used the While command instead of a For...Next loop.

Recursion

A RECURSIVE ALGORITHM is an algorithm that depends on a function calling itself. This is one of the most powerful and elegant types of algorithms that programmers use. Recursion can be a tricky concept to understand—you won't find too many real-life situations that use it. But it is easy to see in some simple mathematical examples.

The *factorial* is a function used often in statistics. The factorial of a number results when you multiply all integers from 1 to that number. For example, the factorial of 5 is calculated by the expression $1 \times 2 \times 3 \times 4 \times 5$ and the result is 120.

The obvious way to implement the factorial function is to use a For...Next loop that multiplies all the values up to the number specified, storing the results in a temporary variable. Function Factorial1 demonstrates this:

```
Function Factorial1 (X As Integer) As Double
    Dim counter As Integer
    Dim result As Double

    result = 1    ' Be sure to initialize to 1
    For counter = 1 To X      ' Loop through each value
        result = result * counter
    Next counter

    Factorial1 = result

End Function
```

The Factorial of a number can also be defined as follows:

If the number is 1, the result is 1.

Otherwise, the result is the number multiplied by the factorial of the number minus 1.

This can be represented by the following recursive function:

```
Function Factorial2 (X As Integer) As Double
    If X = 1 Then
        Factorial2 = 1
    Else
        Factorial2 = X * Factorial2(X - 1)
    End If
End Function
```

The Binary Search

In most cases, if you have an array of information, the only way to find a particular entry is to scan the array from start to finish. Assuming the data is organized randomly, the maximum number of comparisons will equal the length of the array and the average number will equal half the length of the array. However, if the data in the array is sorted, the search time can be shortened dramatically by using recursion and the binary search algorithm.

For an encyclopedia represented by an array called Volumes, where each entry contains the first letter for a volume, a BASIC implementation of the binary search algorithm could look something like this:

```basic
Function BinarySearch (First As Integer, Last As Integer, FindText As String) As Integer
    Dim Halfway As Integer   ' The halfway point
    If First = Last Then
        ' If we found the result, return the volume number
        ' Otherwise, return 0 (not found)
        If volumes(First) = FindText Then BinarySearch = First Else BinarySearch = 0
        Exit Function
    End If

    ' Find the halfway point
    Halfway = (Last - First) \ 2 + First
    If FindText <= volumes(Halfway) Then
        ' Search lower half of the array
        BinarySearch = BinarySearch(First, Halfway, FindText)
    Else ' Search the upper half of the array
        BinarySearch = BinarySearch(Halfway + 1, Last, FindText)
    End If
End Function
```

In this example, the maximum number of comparisons needed with a binary search is five. The real advantage of a binary search comes into play with very large sorted arrays. Each time the function is called, half the array is eliminated from further consideration. A simple loop, on the other hand, compares each entry in the array. An array with 10,000 entries could take up to 10,000 comparisons with a simple scan, but requires no more than 14 comparisons with a binary search.

VOL 1	VOL 2	VOL 3	VOL 4	VOL 5	VOL 6	VOL 7
A	B-C	D-E	F-G	H-I	J-K	L-M

The bars below show parameters First and Last each time the BinarySearch function is called for two different examples. The function continues to call itself until the two parameters are equal.

Search for volume F: BinarySearch(1, 14, "F")

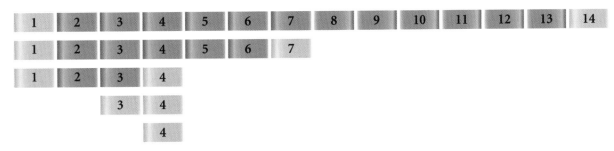

Search for volume R: BinarySearch(1, 14, "R")

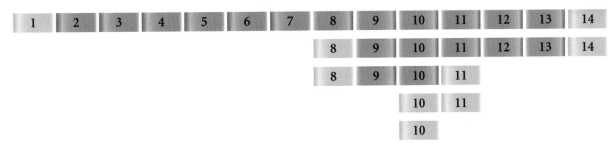

The divide and conquer approach used here can also be used to search for data in a binary tree such as that shown in Chapter 16. The SearchBinaryTree algorithm could be described like this: If the current node is the one you are searching for, return the value of the current node. If the value you are searching for is smaller than the current value, perform the SearchBinaryTree algorithm on the left child node, otherwise perform it on the right child node.

VOL 8	VOL 9	VOL 10	VOL 11	VOL 12	VOL 13	VOL 14
N-O	P-Q	R-S	T	U-V	W-X	Y-Z

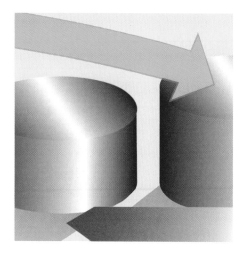

Sorting

T SEEMS THAT every class or book on programming discusses sorting. At first glance, this may seem odd because many programs never need to sort information. However, there are several reasons why it is important to understand how sorting works.

Sorting is necessary for any application that provides output in the form of a report or table because it is far easier for people to interpret sorted data than unsorted data. A database program is a classic example of an application that allows a user to sort information in many different ways.

Programs often sort data internally in order to improve performance. Both the binary search example in Chapter 18 and the fence post example in Chapter 17 depend on an array being sorted. If these arrays weren't sorted, it would be necessary to either sort them first, or develop completely different algorithms that did not depend on the information being in a particular order.

Finally, sorting is a well-defined task for which there exist a great many possible algorithms. As such, sorting is an ideal topic for academic study and a rich source of examples for comparing different programming techniques.

For our purposes we will examine two different sorting algorithms. The *bubble sort* is the easiest sorting algorithm to understand and takes the least amount of code to implement. However, it is also the slowest of the sorting algorithms. The *quick sort* algorithm uses the divide-and-conquer technique introduced in Chapter 18 to obtain excellent performance, and is in fact one of the most popular sorting algorithms. In theory, the quick sort algorithm is one of the fastest algorithms available. In practice, there are many factors to consider that determine which sorting algorithm to use. Among these are the size of the array, type of data, and whether you are sorting on disk or in memory.

The Bubble Sort

The bubble sort works by comparing adjacent entries in the array and swapping them if they are in the wrong order. In effect, the lower numbers "bubble up" to the start of the array. As you will see, each scan through the array allows a value to move up by not more than one space. This means the number of scans through the array can, in the worst case, equal the number of items in the array; thus, the maximum number of comparisons is the size of the array squared.

A simple bubble sort algorithm is shown below:

```
Sub BubbleSort ()
    Dim FoundOne As Integer
    Dim Index As Integer
    Dim TempHolder As Integer
    Do
        ' Each pass begins here
        FoundOne = False
        ' Flag that indicates that at least one pair was
        ' out of order on this pass.
        ' The number of entries to scan is one less
        ' than the length of the array.
        For Index = 1 To 7
            If array(Index) > array(Index + 1) Then
                ' Swap the two values
                TempHolder = array(Index)
                array(Index) = array(Index + 1)
                array(Index + 1) = TempHolder
                ' And note that the array isn't yet sorted
                FoundOne = True
            End If
        Next Index
    Loop While FoundOne ' Continue until sorted
End Sub
```

The following example shows each pass of a bubble sort of an array containing the numbers 17, 4, 8, 24, 1, 13, 7, and 15. The first pass performs the following swaps that lead to the order shown for the start of the second pass.

17	4	4	4	4	4	4
4	17	8	8	8	8	8
8	8	17	17	17	17	17
24	24	24	1	1	1	1
1	1	1	24	13	13	13
13	13	13	13	24	7	7
7	7	7	7	7	24	15
15	15	15	15	15	15	24

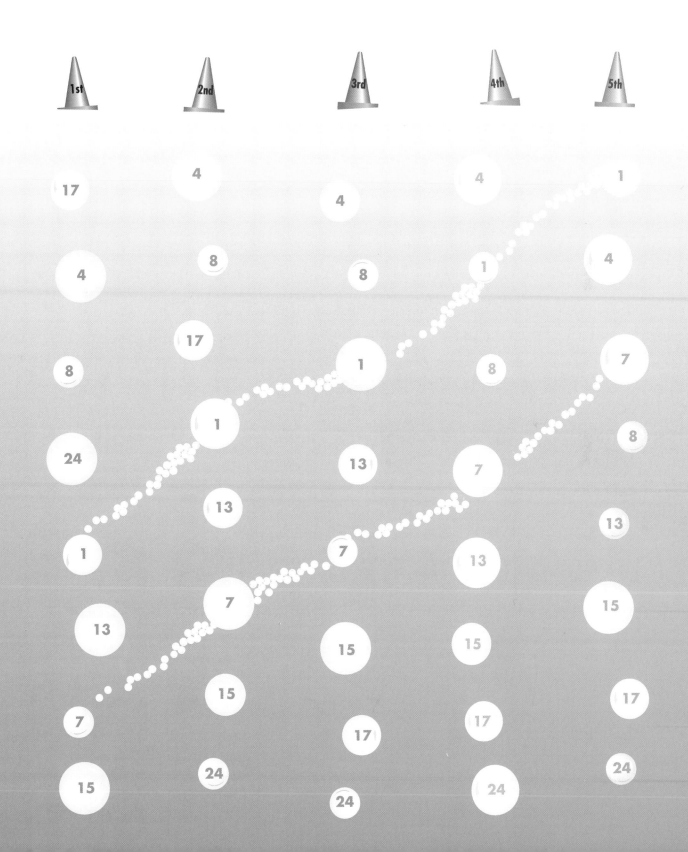

The Quick Sort

The divide-and-conquer technique shown in Chapter 18 can be used with sorting, as well. Let's say you have a series of weights that you want to sort. The binary search algorithm divides the array represented by the weights in half. For the quick sort, imagine that you have a way to divide the weights so that all those in the first half of the array are lighter than all the weights in the second half.

In the first half of the array, the weights are all 13 ounces or lighter. In the second half, they are 14 ounces or heavier. Now, all we need to do is sort the two parts of the array; performing the quick sort algorithm on each part can accomplish this. This sorting process continues until each array has one or two entries. If the two entries are in the wrong order, they are swapped.

The array is now sorted.

Dividing the Array

Dividing the array into two parts is the key to making the quick sort work. Ideally, we would somehow be able to choose the value that would divide the array exactly in half. One half of the array would contain entries smaller than this value and the other half would contain larger entries. However, the process of finding this center value can take as much time as the sorting itself. Fortunately, the quick sort algorithm does not require dividing the array in half; it can be divided anywhere. In this example we simply take the first entry in the array and set it aside, then proceed to divide the rest of the array knowing that ultimately the value 14 will be the dividing point. The following steps illustrate how the array can be divided into two parts. The quick sort algorithm that is described to the left uses this process.

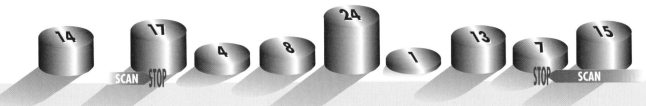

We scan the array from the left and right. On the left, as soon as we find a value that is larger than the first value, we stop. On the right, as soon as we find a value that is smaller than the first value, we stop and swap the two values.

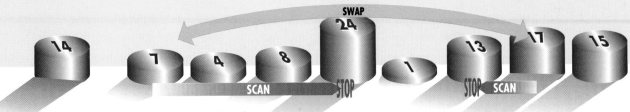

The scanning continues from the previous location.

Once the left and right scan locations meet, we swap the contents of that location with the first entry in the array. In this case, all entries to the left of 14 are smaller than 14, and all entries to the right are greater. Now the left and right sides are quick sorted separately.

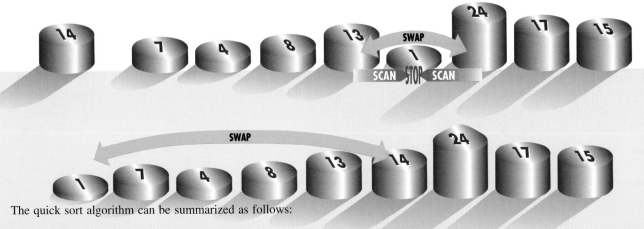

The quick sort algorithm can be summarized as follows:

```
Sub QuickSort(First, Last)
    Dim DividePoint As Integer
    ' You can't sort a single entry array
    if First=Last then exit sub
    ' DivideTheArray is a function that performs the array division
    ' operation described above.
    DividePoint = DivideTheArray(First, Last)
    ' Now we recursively sort the two sides of the array
    QuickSort(First, DividePoint-1)
    QuickSort(First, DividePoint+1)
End Sub
```

Working with Files

ALMOST EVERY APPLICATION provides a mechanism for loading or saving data to and from a computer's hard- or floppy-disk drive. Data on a disk is saved in files, so it is not surprising that every language includes the ability to work with files.

There are dramatic differences in how various languages handle file operations. The file operations in some languages are built into the language itself. Languages such as C and C++ use a library of standard functions to implement file operations; this library is available to the programmer.

The ways in which languages work with files can vary a great deal, but there are some qualities that are common to virtually every language and operating system. For example, each file always has a name and the maximum length of a file's name depends on the operating system. Furthermore, there are several ways in which data can be organized in a file.

Text files hold text that is divided into lines that can have different lengths. Each line is separated from the next by one or two special characters. The most common of these is the *CRLF pair*, which consists of the Carriage Return (ASCII value 13) and Line Feed (ASCII value 10) characters. Most languages or file-function libraries have functions that allow you to read or write data on a line-by-line basis. These functions sometimes automatically strip off the CRLF separator characters during a read operation or automatically add them during a write operation in order to simplify your programs.

Binary files are used to hold any type of data, for example, spreadsheets, image data, documents, digitized sound, and so on. These files allow you to read or write blocks of data that vary in size. The languages and functions used to access a binary file do not perform any automatic modifications to the file's data. Therefore, a programmer must thoroughly understand the structure of a binary file in order to manipulate it correctly.

You can organize a file into fixed-length blocks of binary data. These blocks are often referred to as *records*, each of which typically contains one or more data structures. When a file contains fixed-length records, it is easy to calculate the position of a record in a file by multiplying the number of the record by its size. Many database programs use this technique.

A language or file library will typically contain functions for creating, renaming, and deleting files. There are five types of functions that are usually supported on existing files. Before using a file, you must *open* it. You can then use *input* functions to read data from the file, and *output* functions to write data to the file. A *seek* function allows you to set the position in the file for the next input or output operation. Finally, you perform a *close* operation when you are finished accessing the file.

File Operations

1 You must open a file before you can work on it. Most operating systems allow you to control how a file is opened. You can decide to open a file in text or binary mode, you can allow the program to modify the file or open it for reading only, and so on.

2 Once a file is open, think of it as a very long sheet of paper. You can search through it and read it. You can also write on the paper, changing the data that was previously there.

However, it is difficult to insert data into a file. Just as you can't stretch a sheet of paper, you can't lengthen a file from within. However, you can tape new sheets of paper to the end of the original sheet. Likewise, the only way you can increase the size of a file is by adding space at the end of the file.

3 To insert information into a file, you must first lengthen the file.

insert new data ›

4 Then move the data from the insertion point to the end of the file.

insert new data ›

5 This leaves space within the file where you can write the new data.

space for new data

6 Deleting information from a file reverses this process. In practice, most programs simply delete data by marking the space in the file as free. This is faster than shifting the data in the file.

There is no way to calculate the record location

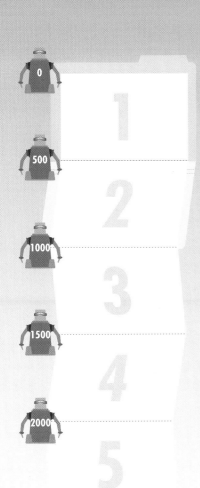

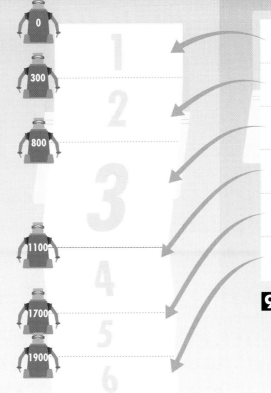

1	0
2	300
3	800
4	1100
5	1700
6	1900

9 It is possible to create complex data files that combine both approaches. For example, you can create one file with fixed-length records where each record contains the location in a second file of the actual record. The second file contains the variable-length record itself. You can then find any record by first looking up its location in the index file.

8 In many cases, each data record has a variable length. Lines of text are a good example of a variable-length record. For example, sentence length can vary considerably. With variable-length records, there is no way to calculate where a particular record will be in a file. So finding or changing a record is a much slower process compared to using files containing fixed-length records. The advantage of using variable-length records is that there is no waste of space—a record always uses exactly as much space as it needs. A record can also always obtain as much space as it needs.

Example

```
Record Length = 500
Record 1 at 0
Record 2 at 500
Record 3 at 1000
Record N at (N-1) x 500
```

7 The file's organization determines how long it takes to find a particular data record. The easiest way to organize a file is to make each record in the file exactly the same size. Once you know exactly how much space each record takes, you can calculate a record's location by multiplying the size by the number of the record. However, there are two disadvantages to using fixed-length records. First, if a particular record does not require all the space allocated, the extra space in the record is wasted. Second, if a particular record requires more space than is allocated, you must either edit the data to fit within the record, or increase the length of every record in the file.

10 Once you are finished working with the file, you must close it. This is especially important with operating systems that do not write all of the data to the file until after it is closed. Some languages will automatically close an open file when your program ends, but it's good practice to do it explicitly.

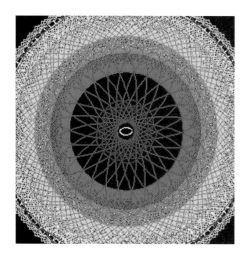

Graphics

THEY SAY a picture is worth a thousand words. Certainly, this book is based on that idea. One of the most exciting developments in the computer world over the past decade has been the appearance of inexpensive, high-quality graphics.

Computer graphics is probably one of the most complex programming subjects. Entire books are written about how to write graphics programs, and about the hundreds of existing graphics algorithms. But as with all programming, the fundamentals are quite simple and accessible even to beginners.

All graphic output falls into one of two categories. Graphics can be built from primitive graphic objects, such as lines and curves. In this case, each element in the graphic can be described by using simple or complex mathematical equations. Graphics can also consist of pictures made up of tiny dots, or *pixels*, each specified by a given color. This type of graphic is also known as a *rasterized* or *bitmap* image.

Most printers and video screens ultimately display a rasterized image—only plotters and very specialized video monitors can display graphics primitives directly. However, many printers, operating systems, and languages provide functions for drawing graphic objects onto raster devices. When they receive a graphics command such as "Line" or "Circle," they automatically draw the object on the device.

From a programmer's point of view, there are usually two types of graphics functions available. There are functions to draw graphics primitives, and there are functions that allow you to manipulate blocks of rasterized image data.

The most common graphics primitives are the line, box, circle, arc, curve, polygon, and fill commands. The most common image functions are the *BitBlt* (short for Bit-Block-Transfer), which copies one area in an image to another, and pixel operations that allow you to set the color for any pixel on the output device.

It is important to note that the operating environment or computer system, not the language itself, usually determines which graphics functions are available to a programmer. This often means that a program written for one operating environment will need to be converted to run on another system, a sometimes difficult task. For example, a C program that uses the graphics library provided with the Microsoft Windows operating environment will require substantial changes to run on an Apple Macintosh. Fortunately, issues of portability are gradually being addressed by system developers. These developers are working on graphics function libraries for use on multiple platforms. These advances will make it increasingly possible to write a single program that will work correctly on many operating systems.

Graphics Programming

Graphics algorithms are among the most mathematically intensive. All the graphic primitive objects, such as lines, circles, curves, polygons, and so on, can be described by using mathematical equations and coordinates. These can be as simple as a line, described by two points, or as complex as a spiral art program that uses trigonometry to generate a complex image.

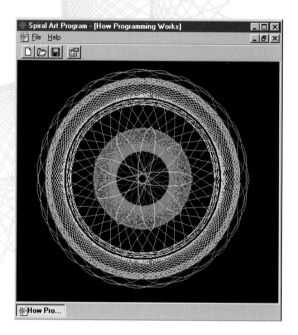

Drawing programs describe objects internally through equations and coordinates. Since the program manipulates graphics data before it is rasterized, it is possible to work with individual graphic objects. In this example, the drawing program converts one object into another by using a complex algorithm called a *morphing* algorithm.

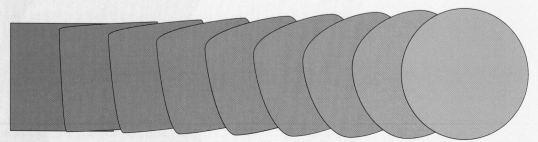

In order to make a graphic object appear on a raster device such as a video screen or printer, it must be rasterized. This is generally accomplished by a library of graphic functions, by the operating system, or by the output device. Here you see a zoomed-in view of what a small circle and line might look like, once rasterized.

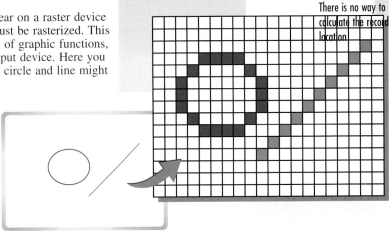

Paint programs differ from drawing programs in that they work directly on the rasterized image, also known as a bitmap. Unlike a drawing program, a paint program does not store individual graphic objects as equations and coordinates. By working with the bitmap, it is able to perform operations such as blends, smears, and image processing that cannot be performed at the graphics-primitive level. Here you see an image that has had its contrast lowered by a paint program.

Coordinate Systems and Drawing

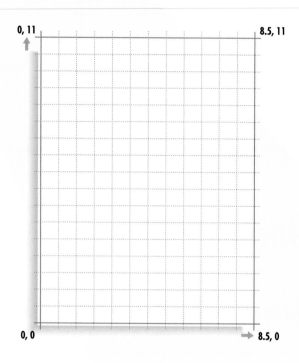

0, 11   8.5, 11

0, 0   8.5, 0

Before you call a function in a graphics library, you have to know something about the coordinate system of the device that you are drawing on. A coordinate system defines the size and units of the display area. For example, the coordinate system for a piece of paper could be defined in inches with the length of the vertical Y axis as 11 inches, and the length of the horizontal X axis as 8.5 inches. It could also be defined as 216 mm by 279 mm. A standard VGA screen uses a pixel coordinate system that is 640 by 480 pixels. However, most graphics libraries allow you to redefine the coordinate system to use units such as inches, millimeters, and so on.

0, 0   640, 0

0, 480   640, 480

Complex images are usually built up from simple objects such as lines, arcs, and rectangles. These objects are defined by their coordinates on the display device. Let's say you have an image made up of a circle and a rectangle. The circle is centered at location 100,100 that has a radius of 40 pixels. The rectangle surrounds it. In Visual Basic you would draw it with the following commands:

```
Dim center As Integer
Dim radius As Integer
center = 100
radius = 40
picture1.Line (center - radius, center - radius)-(center + radius, center + radius), QBColor(3), BF
picture1.Circle (center, center), radius
```

Since the rectangle and circle are built with separate commands, you can manipulate them separately. You can double the size of the circle using simple multiplication, while leaving the rectangle untouched by changing the final line in the listing shown above to the following:

```
picture1.Circle (center, center), radius * 2
```

The image that is created through the drawing can also be manipulated, but only as a single entity; you cannot work with the rasterized circle and rectangle separately. Hereís what happens if you scale the original image by a factor of 2: The resulting image is not as smooth as one that is drawn directly at the desired size because the scaling is accomplished by duplicating pixels.

Simulations

COMPUTER PROGRAMS ALMOST always represent some aspect of reality. The numbers in a spreadsheet might correspond to financial data. Information in a database might describe almost any type of real object from buildings to countries to individuals. But there is a type of computer program where not only does the information in the program correspond to real objects, but the operations that the program itself performs also mimic real-life events. This type of program is called a simulation.

Simulations take many forms. Flight simulators allow you to fly a simulated airplane. Financial simulators can help you plot the course of a business or predict how an investment portfolio might react to changes in the market. Simulations are used extensively in education, allowing students to practice techniques in everything from medicine to stock trading. Simulators can allow you to control cities, planets, surgical procedures, and so on. Whether a leisure game or a serious political simulation, these programs all consist of three parts: a set of data that reflects the desired reality, a set of rules for generating new data based on prior data and user input, and a user interface that lets a user interact with the simulation. The term *virtual reality* is used to describe very sophisticated simulation programs and hardware that are capable of giving you the illusion of being inside a world created by the simulation.

Simulations are important for two main reasons: First, they allow you to safely perform experiments that would be dangerous in the real world. No one has yet died due to the crash of an airplane in a flight simulator. Second, since simulations are computer programs, they can often allow you to try out possibilities more quickly than you could in similar experiments in reality.

Consider the example of rolling a pair of dice. What are the odds of any particular number appearing? A mathematician can derive equations that can be used to calculate this, but it is also possible to determine the odds by rolling the dice several hundred thousand times and counting how many times each number appears. Of course, rolling a pair of dice that many times could be a real problem—unless you simulate the rolls with a computer. Using simulations to solve this type of problem is often called the *Monte Carlo method.*

Simulations and a Trip to Monte Carlo

When writing a simulation, you will usually want your code to correspond as closely as possible to reality. In the case of a dice-rolling simulator, this means randomly choosing a value between one and six for each die, then adding the two values. Choosing a random value between 2 and 12 (the range values that can be achieved by rolling two dice) would not provide an accurate simulation, since the odds of each number appearing varies.

The following BASIC code demonstrates a dice-rolling simulator:

```
Sub DiceRolls (NumberOfRolls As Long)
    ' Define an array to count the totals
    ReDim Values(12) As Integer
    Dim roll As Long
    Dim FirstDie As Integer
     Dim SecondDie As Integer
    Dim TotalRolled As Integer

    For roll = 1 To NumberOfRolls
        ' Roll both dice
        ' Rnd is a function that returns a real number between zero and one.
        FirstDie = Int(Rnd * 6) + 1
        SecondDie = Int(Rnd * 6) + 1
        TotalRolled = FirstDie + SecondDie
        ' Now note the fact that this number was rolled
        Values(TotalRolled) = Values(TotalRolled) + 1
    Next roll

    ' Now print out the results
    For TotalRolled = 2 To 12
        ' Print the value, the number of times the value was rolled,
        ' and the percentage of time that is was rolled
        Print TotalRolled, Values(TotalRolled),
        Print (Values(TotalRolled) / NumberOfRolls) * 100
    Next TotalRolled
End Sub
```

The theoretical odds for each possible roll can be calculated for two dice without a simulation by listing every possible combination of rolls and counting the frequency of appearance of each roll. Divide this frequency by the 36 possible rolls and you have the odds—the percentage of rolls for which a particular value will appear.

With the Monte Carlo method, we simulate a very large number of rolls and add up the number of times each value appears. We then divide that frequency by the total number of rolls to obtain the percentage. The accuracy of this method increases as you increase the total number of rolls because, by nature, statistical calculations deal with very large samples.

Die 1	1	1	1	1	1	1	2	2	2	2	2	2	3	3	3	3	3	3	4	4	4	4	4	4	5	5	5	5	5	5	6	6	6	6	6	6
Die 2	1	2	3	4	5	6	1	2	3	4	5	6	1	2	3	4	5	6	1	2	3	4	5	6	1	2	3	4	5	6	1	2	3	4	5	6
Total	2	3	4	5	6	7	3	4	5	6	7	8	4	5	6	7	8	9	5	6	7	8	9	10	6	7	8	9	10	11	7	8	9	10	11	12

In the case of a dice simulation, it is as easy or easier to do the theoretical calculation as it is to use a simulator, but this is not always the case. Consider the difficulty of simulating the roll of five dice or ten. Simulations are often the best way to characterize complex systems.

Total	Theoretical Frequency	Theoretical Percentage	Dice 1000 Rolls	Percentage	Dice 50000 Rolls	Percentage
2	1	2.8%	32	3.2%	1414	2.8%
3	2	5.6%	57	5.7%	2741	5.5%
4	3	8.3%	85	8.5%	4169	8.3%
5	4	11.1%	120	12.0%	5497	11.0%
6	5	13.9%	146	14.6%	6955	13.9%
7	6	16.7%	163	16.3%	8351	16.7%
8	5	13.9%	135	13.5%	7039	14.1%
9	4	11.1%	120	12.0%	5486	11.0%
10	3	8.3%	67	6.7%	4188	8.4%
11	2	5.6%	57	5.7%	2774	5.5%
12	1	2.8%	18	1.8%	1386	2.8%

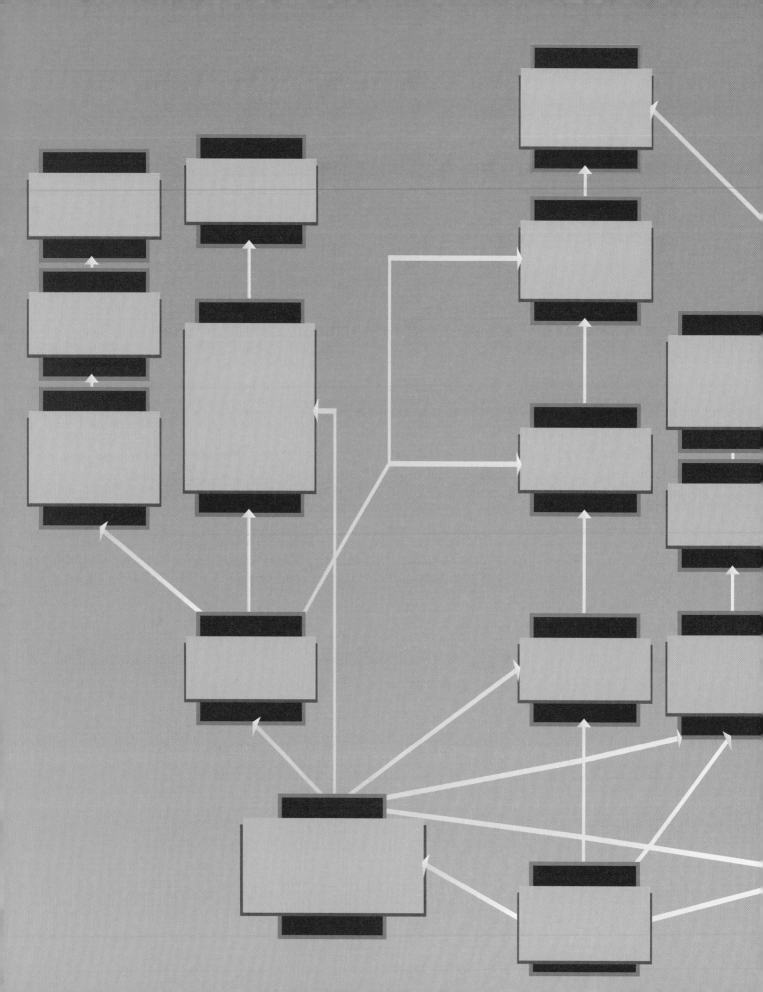

METHODS AND TOOLS

CONTENTS

Chapter 23: How Computer Languages Work
148

Chapter 24: Why Are There So Many
Computer Languages?
152

Chapter 25: How Programmers Work
158

BUILDING A HOUSE is a complex task. First, you need to design the structure—to lay out the locations of the rooms, the doorways, and the various utilities. Once the overall architecture is established, you must go into increasing detail, from specifying the exact dimensions of the walls and materials to deciding where to position the power outlets and phone jacks.

When the design is complete, you need to assemble the materials and do the actual construction. And above all, you must have the right set of tools for the job—you can't build a house with your bare hands.

Constructing a computer program is similar to working on any other construction project. Writing a simple program is as easy as building a paper airplane—neither requires much of a design effort. Writing a large program can be as complex as building a skyscraper.

Up until now, this book has focused on how computer languages are used—how programmers define data structures and create algorithms to perform tasks. These are the raw materials from which a program is constructed. This part focuses on the construction process itself.

The first step in any software project is defining *requirements*. You must answer the following question: What do you want the program to accomplish?

The next step is typically choosing a computer language. Programmers usually choose a language they already know, though this is not always the best choice. Making this decision often includes choosing the tools that comprise the design environment. These tools include editors, compilers, interpreters, debuggers, and so on.

The actual software design usually begins when you are choosing a language. This step is one of the most critical and often neglected parts of the programming process. A strong design can improve all aspects of a program, from its speed to its reliability. It will also improve the likelihood that the final program will fulfill the original requirements.

Coding is the step during which you actually write code. Inexperienced programmers often consider coding the most important programming task. However, in most projects, coding is easier and takes less time than the other tasks.

Documentation is all important. No matter how clear your program may seem at the time you write it, without proper documentation it will be incomprehensible to you a few months later.

Testing and debugging are the processes of taking the code that you have written and making it perform correctly. Hopefully, the code will perform according to the original design, including any modifications made during the design process.

You should also have a good sense of how to manage the various phases of a software project from design to testing.

The most time-consuming tasks in the life of most programs are the ongoing support, maintenance, and enhancements that occur over the long haul.

As you can see, there is a lot more to programming than writing code in a particular language. It is the adherence to these programming steps that marks the real difference between a casual programmer and a professional. Following these steps is a good habit to get into, even for beginners—you will also find yourself learning faster and producing better programs right from the start.

How Computer Languages Work

A CONTRACTOR USES tools to build a house, but how are the tools themselves built? They, too, need to be manufacturedówith other tools.

The most important tool for any programmer is one that can convert program source code that you have written in a particular language into machine language that a computer can actually execute. This tool is itself a program that is said to *implement* a computer language. For example, the program Microsoft Visual C++ is a particular implementation of the C++ language for use with Windows. Microsoft Visual C++ consists of a set of programs that allow you to create a new program written in the C++ language. There are other C++ implementations both for Windows and for other operating systems such as Linux.

There are two major types of computer-language implementations: compilers and interpreters. A *compiler* translates an entire program into machine language. Once translated, a program can execute by itself. An *interpreter* reads your program source code and performs the operations specified without actually translating the code into machine language. The interpreter program executes the program you create, so your program always requires the interpreter.

From the programmer's point of view, there is one great difference between a compiler and interpreter: An interpreter makes it very easy to work with the program interactively, because code is executed one line or statement at a time. You can stop the execution at any point and examine or change both variables and code. With most interpreters you can even type statements one at a time and immediately see the results. Interpreters also tend to make programming easier and speed the testing and debugging processes. The disadvantage of interpreted programs is they tend to execute more slowly than compiled programs, because you are actually executing the interpreter and not a machine-language translation of your program.

There are hybrid approaches that combine compiling and interpreting techniques. Most modern interpreters perform *incremental compilation*, in which your source code is compiled as it is entered into a low-level pseudolanguage called P-Code. The interpreter then executes the P-Code commands.

Some languages, such as C++, Java, Pascal, and Fortran, are almost always compiled. Other languages, such as APL, LISP, LOGO, and Smalltalk, are usually interpreted. BASIC has the distinction of being widely supported by compilers, interpreters, and various hybrid tools.

Communicating at the United Nations

The United Nations has representatives from dozens of countries, speaking many different languages. In order to communicate with each other, they must use translation services.

3 Compilers and interpreters do a lot more than translate your program statements into a form that can be executed. They also maintain a *symbol table*, which is a list of variable names and their locations, and also generate code that allows a language to provide variable types that are not built into the underlying computer hardware. They also control the allocation and management of blocks of memory that your program uses.

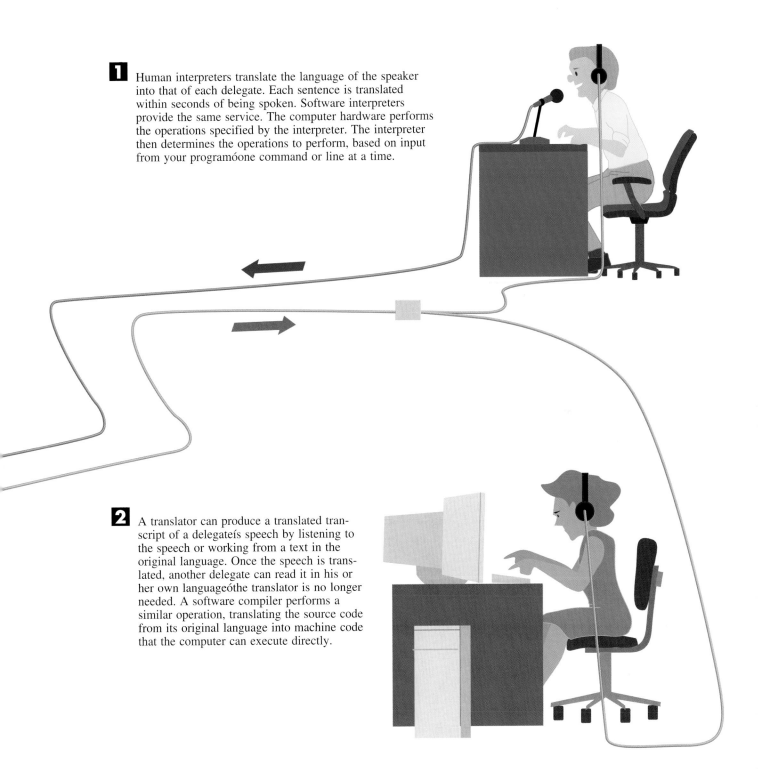

1 Human interpreters translate the language of the speaker into that of each delegate. Each sentence is translated within seconds of being spoken. Software interpreters provide the same service. The computer hardware performs the operations specified by the interpreter. The interpreter then determines the operations to perform, based on input from your programóone command or line at a time.

2 A translator can produce a translated transcript of a delegateís speech by listening to the speech or working from a text in the original language. Once the speech is translated, another delegate can read it in his or her own languageóthe translator is no longer needed. A software compiler performs a similar operation, translating the source code from its original language into machine code that the computer can execute directly.

Why Are There So Many Computer Languages?

DETERMINING WHICH LANGUAGE to use is one of the first decisions that you need to make for any programming project. The natural inclination is to use a language that you already know, but in some cases this choice can end up being the wrong one. As with any task, it is important to use the right tool for the job.

Many factors go into choosing a language. If development time and ease of debugging are more important than execution speed, you may prefer an interpreter to a compiler. If speed is more important, you should choose a compiler. If a program has to achieve the ultimate in performance, you might even choose assembly language. If you want your program to execute on different computers, you should choose a language that is highly standardized, such as Java, C or C++. Novices may prefer to use BASIC which is one of the easier languages to learn.

Most programmers prefer languages that support *structured programming*, which makes it possible to group statements of code into blocks and functions (see Chapter 9). Programmers are also leaning towards languages that support object-oriented programming, which treats data and code as objects (see Chapter 31).

Other questions will arise in the process of selecting a language. Does your language provide all the data types you need? For example, a currency data type is very handy for business applications. Are you working with text? If so, choose a language with powerful functions for working with text strings. Are you programming on a web server? If so PERL or VBScript might be your choice. If you are creating a database, perhaps a language designed for database work, such as SQL or VBA, is appropriate. Does your company require that you use COBOL? Oh well....

Choosing the best language for a task may sound like a complex process, but the choices are not really that overwhelming. Most programmers will do well with one of the popular general-purpose languages, avoiding those that are either obsolete or designed for specialized use.

BASIC remains the most popular language in use today for all but the most performance critical applications. It is especially popular for business applications, and for those who are learning programming. A version of Pascal called Delphi is also a popular choice for general-purpose use.

Java is exciting to many programmers because it promises to make it easy to create programs that will run under any operating system. However, at the time of this printing it has not yet fullfilled that promise, and has a long way to go before it will catch up with either BASIC or C++ in popularity for general programming. However, a language called JavaScript, which is an interpreted language that is based on Java, is by far the most popular language for programming web pages.

C++ is the choice (especially among professional programmers) for high-performance, larger applications that must be portable across different operating systems, and for system-level programming.

And if you are particularly ambitious, it is always possible to create a language of your own.

The Evolution of Computer Languages

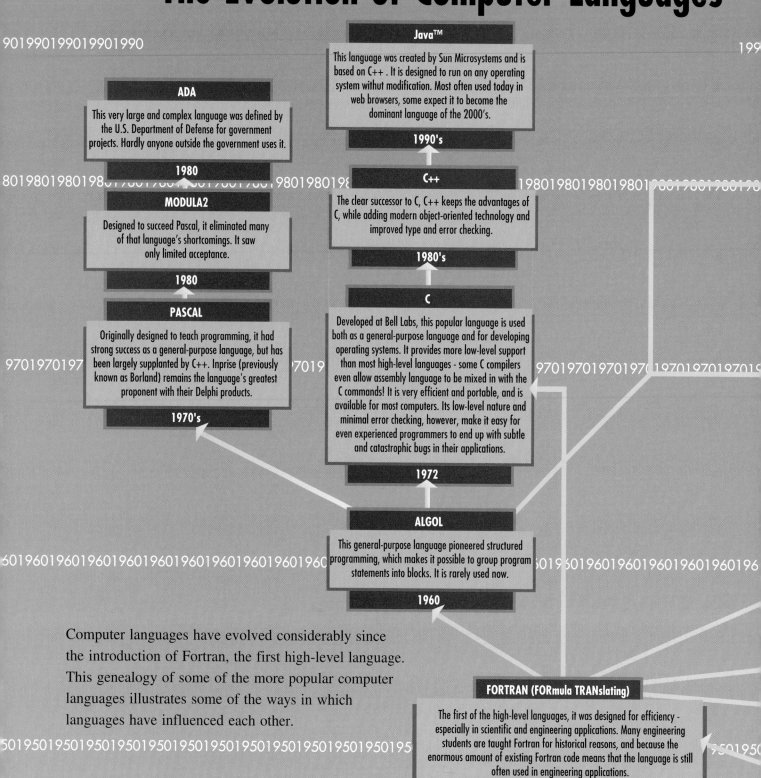

Java™

This language was created by Sun Microsystems and is based on C++ . It is designed to run on any operating system without modification. Most often used today in web browsers, some expect it to become the dominant language of the 2000's.

1990's

ADA

This very large and complex language was defined by the U.S. Department of Defense for government projects. Hardly anyone outside the government uses it.

1980

C++

The clear successor to C, C++ keeps the advantages of C, while adding modern object-oriented technology and improved type and error checking.

1980's

MODULA2

Designed to succeed Pascal, it eliminated many of that language's shortcomings. It saw only limited acceptance.

1980

PASCAL

Originally designed to teach programming, it had strong success as a general-purpose language, but has been largely supplanted by C++. Inprise (previously known as Borland) remains the language's greatest proponent with their Delphi products.

1970's

C

Developed at Bell Labs, this popular language is used both as a general-purpose language and for developing operating systems. It provides more low-level support than most high-level languages - some C compilers even allow assembly language to be mixed in with the C commands! It is very efficient and portable, and is available for most computers. Its low-level nature and minimal error checking, however, make it easy for even experienced programmers to end up with subtle and catastrophic bugs in their applications.

1972

ALGOL

This general-purpose language pioneered structured programming, which makes it possible to group program statements into blocks. It is rarely used now.

1960

Computer languages have evolved considerably since the introduction of Fortran, the first high-level language. This genealogy of some of the more popular computer languages illustrates some of the ways in which languages have influenced each other.

FORTRAN (FORmula TRANslating)

The first of the high-level languages, it was designed for efficiency - especially in scientific and engineering applications. Many engineering students are taught Fortran for historical reasons, and because the enormous amount of existing Fortran code means that the language is still often used in engineering applications.

1957

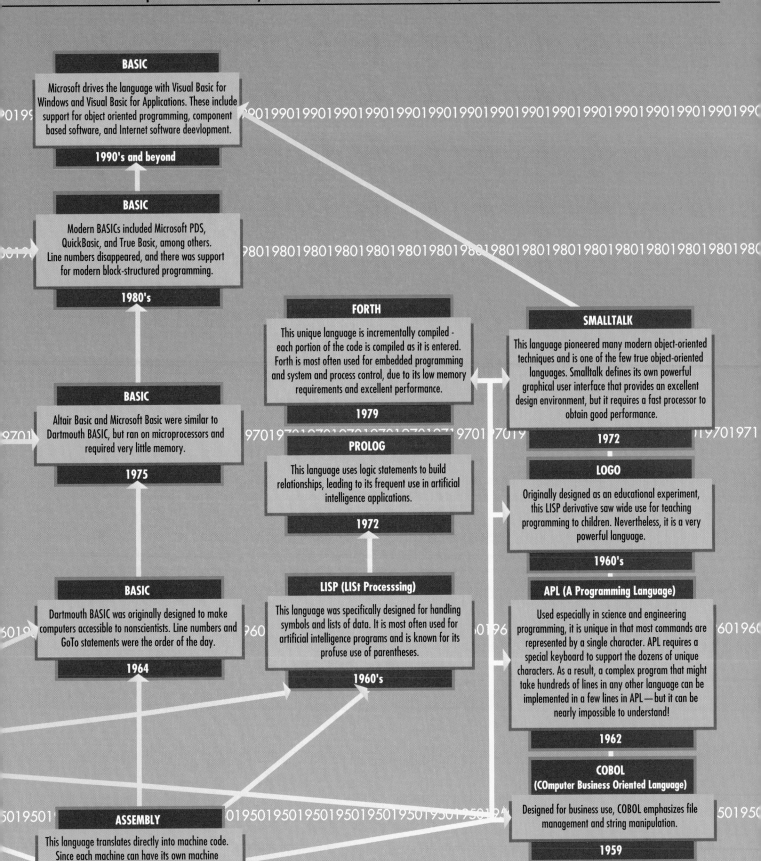

BASIC

Microsoft drives the language with Visual Basic for Windows and Visual Basic for Applications. These include support for object oriented programming, component based software, and Internet software deevlopment.

1990's and beyond

BASIC

Modern BASICs included Microsoft PDS, QuickBasic, and True Basic, among others. Line numbers disappeared, and there was support for modern block-structured programming.

1980's

BASIC

Altair Basic and Microsoft Basic were similar to Dartmouth BASIC, but ran on microprocessors and required very little memory.

1975

BASIC

Dartmouth BASIC was originally designed to make computers accessible to nonscientists. Line numbers and GoTo statements were the order of the day.

1964

ASSEMBLY

This language translates directly into machine code. Since each machine can have its own machine language, there are many different assembly languages.

FORTH

This unique language is incrementally compiled - each portion of the code is compiled as it is entered. Forth is most often used for embedded programming and system and process control, due to its low memory requirements and excellent performance.

1979

PROLOG

This language uses logic statements to build relationships, leading to its frequent use in artificial intelligence applications.

1972

LISP (LISt Processsing)

This language was specifically designed for handling symbols and lists of data. It is most often used for artificial intelligence programs and is known for its profuse use of parentheses.

1960's

SMALLTALK

This language pioneered many modern object-oriented techniques and is one of the few true object-oriented languages. Smalltalk defines its own powerful graphical user interface that provides an excellent design environment, but it requires a fast processor to obtain good performance.

1972

LOGO

Originally designed as an educational experiment, this LISP derivative saw wide use for teaching programming to children. Nevertheless, it is a very powerful language.

1960's

APL (A Programming Language)

Used especially in science and engineering programming, it is unique in that most commands are represented by a single character. APL requires a special keyboard to support the dozens of unique characters. As a result, a complex program that might take hundreds of lines in any other language can be implemented in a few lines in APL—but it can be nearly impossible to understand!

1962

COBOL
(COmputer Business Oriented Language)

Designed for business use, COBOL emphasizes file management and string manipulation.

1959

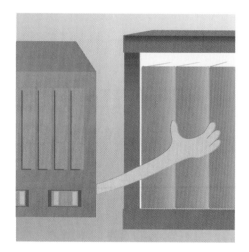

How Programmers Work

EVERY PROGRAMMER BEGINS with an idea—a task to perform or a problem to solve. But programming is more than just solving the problem or performing the task. It is the process of creating a sequence of instructions that a machine can execute in order to perform the task or solve the problem for you.

The first step to accomplishing a programming task is to figure out how you would perform the task yourself. For example, how would you check the spelling of all the words in a document? You would need to identify the words in the text and then look them up in a dictionary. You couldn't possibly program a computer to do this if you couldn't do it yourself.

Once you know how to perform a task yourself, it is possible to design the program. You can divide the spell-checking problem into two parts—identifying each word in the document and looking it up. The data structures the program uses are obvious. There must be one or more string variables to hold the document, and some sort of data structure that contains the list of words in the dictionary. The dictionary could be in the form of a sorted array of strings, though in practice it is possible to create more efficient data structures for this purpose.

You also need to choose algorithms for the program. Finding the individual words in the text can be a complex process. You must consider how to handle punctuation, spaces, capitalization, and whether to strip off suffixes such as "ing," and "ed." These tasks are easy for humans, but you will have to specify exactly how to perform these operations if you want your program to perform them. You will also need to choose a searching algorithm for your dictionary that is fast enough to be practical.

There are two remaining tasks that you should tend to in order to complete the design process: You should define your program's user interface and create high-level documentation. The documentation should describe the overall operation of the program. After the design is complete, it is time to write the code. Be sure to document the program as you write it, placing comments in the code listings.

Testing and debugging involve using the program and trying to make it fail. Debugging is detective work. The program's behavior gives you the clues, and you need to deduce from them what is happening within the program that can cause that behavior. Debugging tools can help by providing you with the values of variables as the program is running. These tools can also trace the course of the program and list the functions that are called and their parameters.

The sequence of designing, coding, testing, and debugging sounds good in theory. However, in practice, software development is not that straightforward. Frequently, issues arise during coding and testing that can cause you to change the design of the program. As the program begins to take shape, you'll often find that features that seemed like a good idea don't work well in practice, and that you have better ideas to replace them. There will also be cases where you will redesign and recode part of your program to improve performance.

In a business environment, specific issues come into play: you may need to consider creating help files and operating manuals, providing customer support, testing the program on different system configurations, and so on. Finally, there is always the temptation to add just one more feature—sometimes making it seem that no program is ever really complete.

Designing a Program

1 There are many ways to design a program, but the first step is usually to figure out the requirements of the program; determine exactly what you want the program to do. In this example, the requirement is to add a sequence of numbers from 1 to a number specified by the user.

2 One of the traditional ways of designing programs is to use a flowchart. The top of the flowchart indicates input from the user. Rectangles contain statements and diamonds indicate decisions.

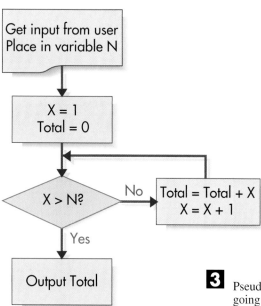

3 Pseudocode allows you to describe the operation of the program without going into detail and worrying about following the syntax of any particular computer language.

```
Function AddSequence
  Integer N, X, Total       ' Three integer variables
  N = Get a number from the user
  For X = 1 to N      ' Loop through the values 1 through N
        Total = Total + X
  Next X
  Return Total
End Function AddSequence
```

4 There are many other techniques for designing complex programs. In fact, there are programs that can help you to design software and keep track of the flow of data through the various components of your application. These software-engineering tools are most frequently used for large projects that involve many programmers.

5 One common approach to developing applications is called *top-down design*. This involves creating a hierarchy of functions for your program. The top functions closely reflect the requirements of the program. You then define the functions that will be called by these top-level functions, moving down the hierarchy to the lowest-level functions. When it is time to write the actual code, you start by coding the lowest-level functions and work your way up.

This example illustrates the hierarchy of functions that might be used by a washing machine.

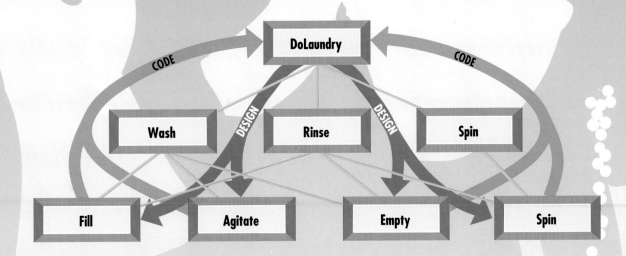

6 *Prototyping* is one of the best design techniques for testing out a program's user interface. Unlike earlier prototyping tools that could only design screens, modern programming environments let you build on the user interface to create your final program. Many high-level languages, including C++, Smalltalk, and Visual Basic, include powerful user-interface design tools that allow you to position objects such as buttons and text fields on the screen to see how the application will look and behave when it is complete. This user interface for a washing-machine program took less than five minutes to create using Visual Basic.

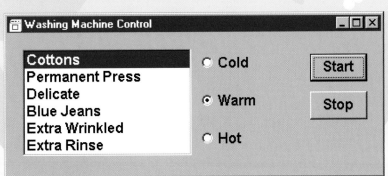

Coding and Documentation

1 Coding starts with a programmer working at a computer. The most important tool for a programmer is an *editor*, a program that creates text files called *source code modules*. An editor is like a word processor, except that it is optimized for programming. For example, it might display language commands in one color and comments in another to make it easier to see the structure of the program. Additional tools can be used to create other program components such as bitmaps or icons.

2 A compiler translates each text file into machine code and places it in an object file. A computer can only execute machine code. However, an object file is not entirely ready for execution. Some of the locations for variables and functions have not yet been assigned, because they may be in a different object file.

3 A program called a *linker* combines all the object files into an executable program that can run directly on the target computer.

4 An interpreter works somewhat differently. The interpreter program itself is executed by the computer. This program reads text from the source file and performs the operations specified by the commands in that file.

SOURCE TEXT FILE

SOURCE TEXT FILE

Interpreter

5 Coding standards are very important. Use variable names that describe the contents of the variable and function names that describe the behavior of the function. Indent blocks of text so that you can easily see where a block begins and ends. Lastly, document your code as you write it by including comments.

There are a number of other tools available that operate on source code modules. Listing programs create printed listings of the code that are made more readable by indentation and other text formatting. Cross-reference programs analyze the source code and list all the variables and functions used by the program and where they are accessed. Class browsers list all the structures in an object-oriented program, the functions associated with them, and where they are used.

TEXT MODULE

TEXT MODULE

TEXT MODULE

TEXT MODULE

COMPILER

6 A *librarian* is a program that combines object files into a single file called a *library*. Large programs can contain hundreds or thousands of source files. Rather than try to keep track of them individually, it is common for a programmer to place them in a library. Linkers are able to extract object modules from libraries automatically, as needed. Source Code Control systems do the same for source files, and allow you to track changes and versions of your program.

OBJECT FILE

OBJECT FILE

OBJECT FILE

OBJECT FILE

LINKER

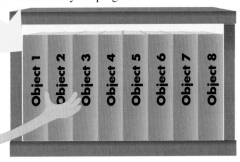

EXECUTABLE FILE

EXECUTABLE FILE

7 A *profiler* is a program that analyzes a program while it is running and determines how much time is being spent in each function in the program. It is a rule of thumb that 90 percent of the time in a program is spent executing less than 10 percent of the code. This is because most of the time in your program is spent in loops or in functions that are frequently called during the course of executing the program. A profiler identifies these time-consuming routines so that you can concentrate on improving their performance, providing the best overall performance increase.

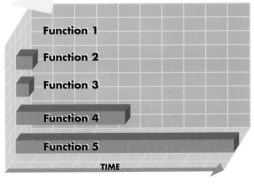

Function 1
Function 2
Function 3
Function 4
Function 5
TIME

Testing and Debugging

1 In the story *The Sorcerer's Apprentice*, a young apprentice wizard, too lazy to carry in the water himself, magically forces a broom to carry the water for him. In effect, he programs the broom as follows (in pseudocode):

```
Function BringWater
DoItAgain:    ` A label marking the start of the function
     Go Outside
     Fill Bucket With Water
     Come Inside
     Pour Water Into Tub
 Goto DoItAgain
End Function
```

2 The apprentice, confident that the tub will soon be filled, falls asleep. Meanwhile, the broom continues to bring the water in even after the tub has been filled. If the apprentice had read this book, he would have realized that there was a bug in his program: There is no way to cause the function to stop.

3 In the original story, the apprentice tries to stop the broom by hacking at it with an ax. Unfortunately, this attempt at a system reboot fails and instead causes the function BringWater to be called again and again, as each splinter formed a new broom that brings in even more water.

4 In our story, however, the apprentice is able to find a copy of *How Computer Programming Works* and quickly realizes what has caused the error in his program. He rewrites it as follows:

```
Function BringWater
     Do ' Beginning of a block to execute until Loop statement
          Go Outside
          Fill Bucket With Water
          Come Inside
          Pour Water Into Tub
     Loop While(Not TubFilled)   ' If tub isnít filled, go to Do
                                 ' statement
     CrawlIntoCorner          ' Put broom away when done
End Function
```

The broom realizes instantly that the tub is filled, crawls into a corner, and returns to broomlike behavior.

5 A large part of programming consists of simulating the performance of a program in your head—thinking about what the computer will do at each step in the program. This is essential for debugging, where a simple oversight can lead to a catastrophic failure in your code.

Legend has it that program glitches began to be called bugs after it was discovered that a program failure on one of the early tube-based computers was caused by a moth getting into the wiring.

Murphy's law of programming states that no nontrivial program is free of bugs. A corollary states that any program with more than ten lines is by definition nontrivial. The bottom line—your program will have bugs. A strong design and good coding techniques will reduce their number and help you to find them quickly.

LANGUAGE AND TECHNOLOGIES

CONTENTS

Chapter 26: How Assembly Language Works
172

Chapter 27: How the C Language Works
178

Chapter 28: How BASIC Works
182

Chapter 29: How Event-Driven Programming Works
188

Chapter 30: How User Interface Design Works
192

Chapter 31: How Object-Oriented, Component, and
Client-Server Programming Works
198

Chapter 32: How Internet Programming Works
206

Chapter 33: How Embedded Programming Works,
and How to Program Your VCR
212

AUTOMOBILES HAVE EVOLVED quite a bit since Model T Fords first appeared. Some aspects of this evolution are obvious. For example, modern cars no longer sport the fins and large chrome grills of the 1950s. However, other developments, such as automatic transmissions, fuel injection, and antilock brakes, are more subtle. They are a few of the less visible improvements of the past few decades.

Though they have not been around as long as cars, computers have developed at a breakneck pace. The computer you buy today is hundreds of times faster than what was available a decade ago, and it is also far less expensive. The changes that have occurred in programming technology are less apparent, but equally remarkable. The 1990's saw a dramatic change from terminal-style software that conveys information using lines of text, to fully graphical software that uses mouse cursors, icons, and full-color graphics to provide an operating environment that is vivid and easy to use. The 2000's look like they will continue the trend towards distributed software-programs that run on multiple computers that are tied together by networks such as the Internet.

This closing Part 7 of the book examines several of the most popular languages and newer technologies that you are likely to run into as a programmer. The very last chapter of this book covers the one programming task you are most likely to face, which doesn't even involve sitting down in front of a computer: programming your video cassette recorder (VCR). You will find that, given your new understanding of programming, this perhaps intimidating task will become simple and routine.

How Assembly Language Works

ASSEMBLY LANGUAGE is the lowest level of programming that you are likely to encounter. Each instruction in assembly language corresponds to a single instruction for a *central processing unit* (CPU). A program called an *assembler* translates your assembly language commands into the numbers that your computer hardware can execute. Since assembly language is closely involved with the CPU hardware, every type of CPU has its own unique assembly language, though some CPUs are intentionally designed to execute all or part of the instruction set of another CPU.

To use assembly language, it is necessary that you understand a little bit about how computers work internally. A high-level language allows you to declare and work with variables, without knowing where or how these variables are stored, and will typically handle all aspects of allocating space for those variables. It can also support user-defined variables and types of variables the hardware does not support directly. In most cases, assembly language programmers specify the location and order of variables in memory, and are limited to types of variables that the CPU itself can manipulate.

Assembly language programmers must also work with *registers*, a special type of memory that is built into the CPU itself. Registers come in many types and sizes, depending on the hardware. The CPU can access registers much more quickly than it can access the computer's main memory. This means a complex operation will usually involve loading data from memory into registers, performing operations on the registers, and then writing the results back into memory.

There are several types of registers that are common to most CPUs. Most CPUs have at least one *accumulator*, which is also sometimes referred to as a *data register* or a *general purpose register*. Accumulators support all of the fundamental arithmetic and Boolean operations and are used for calculations and for temporary storage of information. The number of bits in these registers determines the width of the processor; thus a CPU with 32-bit-wide data registers is called a 32-bit processor.

Each bit in a *flag register* has a different meaning and is set according to the operation of the CPU. For example, the zero bit indicates when the result of the most recent arithmetic operation was zero. Flags were discussed earlier in Chapter 6.

There are three types of registers that are also pointers. An *address register* is a pointer that contains memory locations. It may support address calculations as well. An *instruction pointer* (IP) is a special address register that tells the CPU the location in memory of the next instruction to execute. A *stack pointer* is a special address register that tells the CPU the location of the top of the CPU stack. Most CPUs provide instructions for implementing a stack in memory that is used for parameter passing and for storing the return address on subroutine calls. Stacks were discussed earlier in Chapter 14.

Few applications today are written entirely in assembly language. In most cases, it is used for only parts of a program where performance is absolutely critical. Unlike most other languages, assembly allows you to optimize your code to obtain the best possible speed by deciding what data to keep in registers at a given time. Although higher-level languages have special built-in optimizing algorithms that use CPU registers efficiently, they can't achieve the same performance as assembly language in the hands of a good programmer. Of course, the price for such performance is hard work, since it is more difficult and more time consuming to program in assembly language than in high-level languages.

Assembly Language

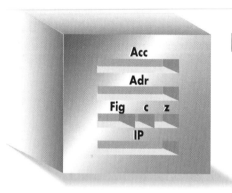

1 Using a language such as BASIC to add two variables is this easy: Result = VarA + VarB. Let's take a look at the assembly language version of this operation on an imaginary 8-bit CPU that can access only 256 bytes of memory and has only the four registers shown.

2 Imagine a CPU that has a few machine language instructions. Each instruction consists of a number that represents a command that the CPU understands how to execute, and an assembly language name.

A program called an assembler converts the assembly language into machine code. Your assembly language program consists of a text file that contains assembly language names, and special commands such as the DB command that are instructions to the assembler. The assembler reads the text file and translates it into machine code, which it loads into consecutive locations in memory.

It is important to understand the difference between a command that produces machine code and a command to the assembler. Commands to the assembler tell the assembly program to perform an operation during the assembly process—for example, to allocate space in memory or to output a program listing. These commands do not appear in the final executable file. Modern macro assemblers can have many powerful assembler commands that make assembly language programming easier.

Number	Name	Description
1	Add	The contents of the memory location that Adr points to is added to Acc.
2	Load	Loads Acc with the contents of the memory location pointed to by Adr.
3	Store	Stores the contents of Acc in the memory location pointed to by Adr.
4,N	LoadA, N	Loads Adr with the value N. The memory location after the command (4) contains the value N.
	DB N = X	Tells assembler to allocate memory for a variable. Does not produce machine code, but simply leaves an empty space in memory. N is the number of bytes to allocate. X is the initial value to load into the allocated space.

Address	Value	Assembly	Description
100	5	VarA: DB 1=5	VarA is at this address
101	9	VarB: DB 1=9	VarB is at this address
102	0	Result: DB 1=0	Result will be at this address
103	4	LoadA, VarA	First of two bytes of LoadA command
104	100		Adr now points to VarA
105	2	Load	Load Acc with VarA; Acc is now 5
106	4	LoadA, VarB	First of two bytes of LoadA command
107	101		Adr now points to VarB
108	1	Add	Adds Acc with VarB; Acc is now 14
109	4	LoadA, Result	First of two bytes of LoadA command
110	102		Adr now points to Result
111	3	Store	Stores Acc to Result; Result is now 14

3 Let's assume that VarA contains the value 5 and is found at address 100 in memory, and VarB contains the value 9 and is found at address 101. Variable Result, at address 102, can be loaded with VarA plus VarB using the assembly language program (shown here) that starts at location 103. This program resembles a typical listing produced after the assembler has converted your program to machine language. The Assembly column contains the assembly language program itself.

NOTE Assembly language is not always the lowest-level language; rather, it is only the lowest level available to programmers using a particular CPU. The CPU itself often contains an even lower level of code called *microcode*. This is the language that controls the internal operation of the CPU itself, and is typically used solely by the manufacturer.

4 The actual executable file for this function would contain a start address that is set by the programmer. The operating system would start by loading the IP register with the starting address. Here you can see the contents of the CPU registers as we trace through the first few statements in this program.

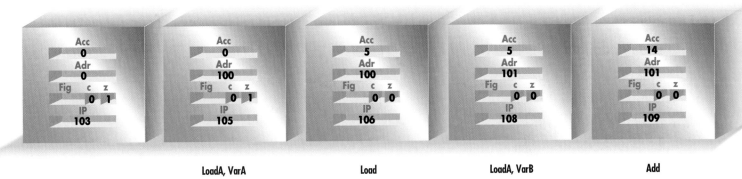

| | LoadA, VarA | Load | LoadA, VarB | Add |

5 As you can see, it took six assembly language statements to perform this simple addition, versus a single line in BASIC. But each one takes very little space in memory and performs far more quickly than the equivalent BASIC statement. A BASIC interpreter might actually perform thousands of machine instructions to perform the same operation. This is because it must analyze the code, find the variables in memory, and finally perform the operation.

6 What if you wanted to add two 16-bit numbers? The assembly language code to add two 16-bit variables might look as shown here as we add the hex values H685 and H182. (Data values are shown in hexadecimal to show the division into two 8-bit bytes. They use the carry flag to indicate that the result of an addition does not fit in the available space, just as you "carry" numbers when doing long addition, and the result for a column is greater than 9. See Chapter 6 for a review of hexadecimal operations.)

As you can see, the need to break the addition into two 8-bit bytes adds many instructions to the program. The extra instructions would not be necessary if you were using a 16-bit processor, one where the internal registers are 16 bits wide. This is one of the reasons performance improves with bus width. By the way, there is a bug in this listing: If the carry flag were set to 1 at the beginning of the routine, the final result would be incorrect. A correct routine would force the carry flag to 0 before the addition operation began.

Address	Value	Assembly	Description
100	H685	VarA: DB 2 = H685	VarA is at this address; 2 bytes now
102	H182	VarB: DB 2 = H182	VarB is at this address
104	0	Result: DB 2 = 0	Result will be at this address
106	4, 101	LoadA, VarA+1	Adr now points to low byte of VarA
108	2	Load	Load Acc, which is now H85
109	4, 103	LoadA, VarB+1	Adr now points to low byte of VarB
111	1	Add	Adds Acc with low byte of VarB; Acc is now 7, and the C (carry) flag is set to one
112	4, 105	LoadA, Result+1	Adr now points to low byte of Result
114	3	Store	Stores Acc to low byte of Result, which is now 7
115	4, 100	LoadA, VarA	Adr now points to high byte of VarA
117	2	Load	Load Acc, which is now H6
118	4, 102	LoadA, VarB	Adr now points to high byte of VarB
120	1	Add	Adds Acc with high byte of VarB; adds one because carry flag is set; Acc is now 8
121	4, 104	LoadA, Result	Adr now points to high byte of Result
123	3	Store	Stores Acc to high byte of Result, which is now H807

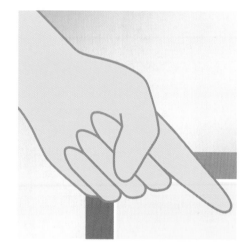

How the C Language Works

MANY BUSINESS PROGRAMMERS use COBOL. Engineers have traditionally programmed in Fortran. Professors teach every language under the sun (sometimes the more obscure, the better), and it seems that everyone programs in BASIC. But when it comes to serious computer scientists, odds are they are using C++. This is true whether they are writing operating systems, compilers, interpreters, games, simulations, word processors, spreadsheets, project managers or virtually anything else. However, C++ is built on the C language, and learning some C is an essential first step to learning C++ (which will be discussed further in chapter 31).

Dennis Ritchie designed C in 1972 as a tool to develop the UNIX operating system, one of the more popular workstation operating systems still in use today. The C language has two great strengths: First, it is a highly transportable language; you can write C software on one computer and quickly recompile it to run on another computer. And the C language is in a sense both a high-level and a low-level language at the same time; herein lies its other strength.

Low-level languages provide excellent performance, but require extra effort on the part of the programmer to work closely to the underlying hardware capabilities. At the low level, C lets you directly access memory locations and even influence the allocation of CPU registers for data. C supports Boolean operations such as bit shifts, which are essential to arithmetic operations and graphic operations. With most versions of C, you can call functions written in assembly language directly, enabling you to use assembly for hardware-dependent or time-critical routines.

High-level languages provide extra capability by handling details such as memory management. They also provide high-level instructions that translate into many lower-level instructions, but this takes a toll on performance. C does both. At the same time, C lets you create well-structured code, supports most numeric types, and provides a versatile set of commands. Most implementations of C also come with a large library of functions derived from the original function library created for UNIX. These libraries provide memory management, file management, and other high-level capabilities. You can purchase additional libraries of functions for use with most popular versions of C.

This mix of low- and high-level capabilities makes C the ideal compromise for a wide variety of projects that require both the programming efficiency of a high-level language and the performance of assembly.

The C Language

A large part of the power of C is due to its support for pointers. A pointer variable in C is defined using the * character. Thus

char *ptr;

creates a variable named ptr that contains the location of a character. You can define a variable that holds a character using the declaration

char c;

You can set variable ptr to point to character c using the address operator, the & character as follows:

ptr = &c;

You can now set the value of variable c in two ways:

c = 5;

or

*ptr = 5;

But beware! If you forget to set variable ptr to point to a variable or another valid memory location before you try to use it, your program can crash. An uninitialized pointer can contain any value. For instance, if ptr pointed to a location in memory containing code, even operating system code, assigning data to that location could cause an incorrect or invalid instruction to be executed—a sure way to halt your system.

One of the prices programmers pay for C's high performance is in error checking. Runtime error checking by the language takes time—and C programmers would rather spend that time executing their programs. As a result, an error that would be detected and identified in another language might be ignored in C, at least until the program crashes. Unfortunately, C allows you to happily overwrite other variables, code, and on some systems, even the operating system itself. Fortunately, C compilers usually come with special programs called *debuggers* that can help track down these problems.

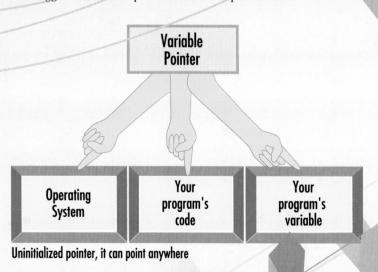

Variable Pointer

Operating System

Your program's code

Your program's variable

Uninitialized pointer, it can point anywhere

DANGER BEWARE DANGLING POINTERS

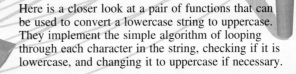

Here is a closer look at a pair of functions that can be used to convert a lowercase string to uppercase. They implement the simple algorithm of looping through each character in the string, checking if it is lowercase, and changing it to uppercase if necessary.

```c
int IsCharLowerCase(char c)
{
    int result;
    if(c >= 'a' && c<='z') result = 1;
    else result = 0;
    return(result);
}


VOID MakeStringUpperCase
(char * ptrToString)
{
    char *cptr;

    cptr = ptrToString;

    while(*cptr) {
        if(IsCharLowerCase(*cptr)) {
            *cptr = *cptr - 32;
        }
        cptr = cptr+1;
    }
    return;
}
```

Functions, like variables, have types. In this case, function IsCharLowerCase is defined to return an integer. The function takes a character as a parameter, which will be named C. Notice that all C statements are in lowercase letters.

The if command in C tests a condition that you must enclose in parentheses. Because of the parentheses, you don't need a Then statement to mark the end of the condition (a requirement in BASIC). The && operator is a Boolean AND operator. In this case, the result is set to TRUE (nonzero) if c is between the letters a and z (lowercase).

Blocks in C are enclosed in brackets. A function is one way to group a block of code. Each statement within a block must end with a ; (semicolon) character.

The VOID function type defines a subroutine that has no return value. The parameter passed here is a pointer to a character. Strings in C are passed using character pointers. The pointer references the first character in the string. The string is terminated with a character with the value zero.

We create a temporary variable cptr that will be used to scan through the string one character at a time. It is initialized to point to the ptrToString parameter.

A character with the value zero marks the end of a string. Any nonzero character needs to be checked. Since the TRUE condition is defined as nonzero, we can simply place the value of the character as the conditional. This is the same as saying while(*cptr!=0). C has many such shortcuts. You'll also notice a bracket that opens a new block. Every statement within this block will be executed each time the while condition is TRUE.

We can use the * operator to refer to the character that is pointed to. The lowercase characters have an ASCII value 32 greater than their corresponding uppercase character, so the uppercase conversion is a simple subtraction.

We set the pointer to point to the next character at the end of the block. C also has a ++ operator that increments a pointer, so we could have used the command cptr++ instead of cptr= cptr+1.

This bracket marks the close of the block opened with the while statement. Notice that blocks can be placed within other blocks.

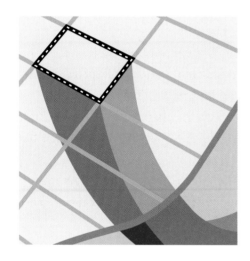

CHAPTER
28

How BASIC Works

IT'S EVERYWHERE. It is the single most popular computer language and perhaps the most hated. It's available for virtually every computer system. It is a beginner's language that is used by professionals. It's used for small projects and large commercial products. It is BASIC. Aside from C++, BASIC is perhaps the most important language in use today.

Many serious programmers look upon BASIC with disdain, and until very recently this response was well deserved. Previous versions of BASIC had limited capability, were very slow, and did not promote or even support modern structured programming techniques. Today's BASIC has eliminated many of these limitations, while preserving its traditional characteristic ease of use. It is most often used with interpreters, though BASIC compilers are also available and provide the fast performance characteristic of compiled programs.

BASIC is also known for its ability to manipulate string variablesómuch more competently than C or Pascal. A built-in currency data type is available in many BASIC implementations. These capabilities make BASIC a good language for business applications.

On the negative side, BASIC continues to be one of the least standardized languages. A program written for one implementation of BASIC on a particular system is unlikely to work correctly on a different implementation of BASIC, even on the same system.

Two developments in the 90's renewed interest in the BASIC language. One was the appearance of Microsoft's Visual Basic language (an implementation of BASIC) that for the first time made programming a PC under the Microsoft Windows environment accessible to beginning and intermediate programmers. Secondly, BASIC has been incorporated into many applications as a high-level macro language. Thus you can now use BASIC to program your word processor, spreadsheet, or other application.

Basic is now becoming increasingly popular as a language for development of software components and Internet application development. You'll read more about that in chapters 31 and 32.

It's Not Your Grandad's BASIC

I started using BASIC in 1964. It had line numbers. We had goto's everywhere and we liked it! It took real programming skill to keep track of subroutines by line number—no wimpy function names for us. Variable names had only one letter and maybe a number. We had global variables only and we loved it! You spoiled kids with your block structures don't know what programming is really like. Here's my favorite routine for converting a string to uppercase. It starts running at line 200.

```
10 REM Set Variable B to 1 if
// value of C is lowercase.
20 IF C >= ASC("a") THEN GOTO 40
30 GOTO 90
40 IF C <= ASC("z") THEN GOTO 60
50 GOTO 90
60 B = 1
70 GOTO 100
90 B = 0
100 RETURN: REM End of subroutine
// to check C for lowercase.
200 REM Subroutine to loop through
// characters in string S$.
210 X = 1
215 IF X > LEN(S$) THEN GOTO 390
// REM reached end of string
220 C = ASC(MID$(S$, X, 1)):
// REM Get Character at location X
230 GOSUB 10
240 IF B = 1 THEN GOTO 260
250 GOTO 300
260 REM It's a lower case character
270 MID$(S$, X, 1) = CHR$(C - 32):
// REM set character to upper
300 X = X + 1
310 GOTO 215
390 RETURN
```

The arrows at the left show the possible flow of instructions in the program. BASIC programs used to have so many jumps that any attempt to trace the flow of the program wound up looking like a bowl of spaghetti— hence the term *spaghetti code* to describe an unstructured program with too many jumps. Purists will note that many older versions of BASIC did not support the use of Mid$ to assign the value of a character.

Dude! That old BASIC is lame—nobody programs like that anymore. Today's BASIC is as good as any other modern language, with local variables, block structures, long variable and function names, and anything else you need. Here's the case conversion program written in modern BASIC:

```
' IsCharLowerCase works with the ASCII
' value of the character
Function IsCharLowerCase (c As Integer) As Integer
    Dim result As Integer
    If c >= Asc("a") And c <= Asc("z") Then
            result = 1
    Else
            result = 0
    Endif
    IsCharLowerCase = result
End Function
Sub MakeStringUpperCase (StringToConvert As String)
    Dim position As Integer
    Dim charvalue As Integer
    position = 1
    While position <= Len(StringToConvert)
        ' Mid$ accesses the character at the
        ' specified position
        ' Asc returns the ASCII value of a
        ' character
        charvalue = Asc(Mid$(StringToConvert, position, 1))
        If IsCharLowerCase(charvalue) Then
            ' Function Chr$ converts an ASCII value into a string
            Mid$(StringToConvert, position, 1) = Chr$(charvalue - 32)
        End If
        position = position + 1
    Wend
End Sub
```

BASIC has a very rich set of commands, especially when it comes to manipulating strings. Most BASIC implementations have a function named UCase$ that converts a string to uppercase, making both of the approaches shown here unnecessary.

Programming an Application

1 Programming is not the most common use for computers. Most people spend the bulk of their computer time using word processors, spreadsheets, telecommunications programs, drawing programs, and a myriad of other types of applications that are useful in daily life.

Many of these applications have programming capability in the form of *macros*. Initially, macro capability involved the recording of keystroke sequences that could be "played back" to perform repetitive operations. Gradually, macro support in some applications evolved into full-featured programming languages, but these languages are often limited due to their roots as keystroke recorders. One of the most exciting developments in recent time has been the appearance of full-featured programming environments as part of an application. These programming environments often include the language, editor, debugger, and even visual programming tools to help you lay out the look of your screen.

Suppose you want to grade students on a curve. You could write a specialized grading program, but a more reasonable approach would be to use a spreadsheet as shown here.

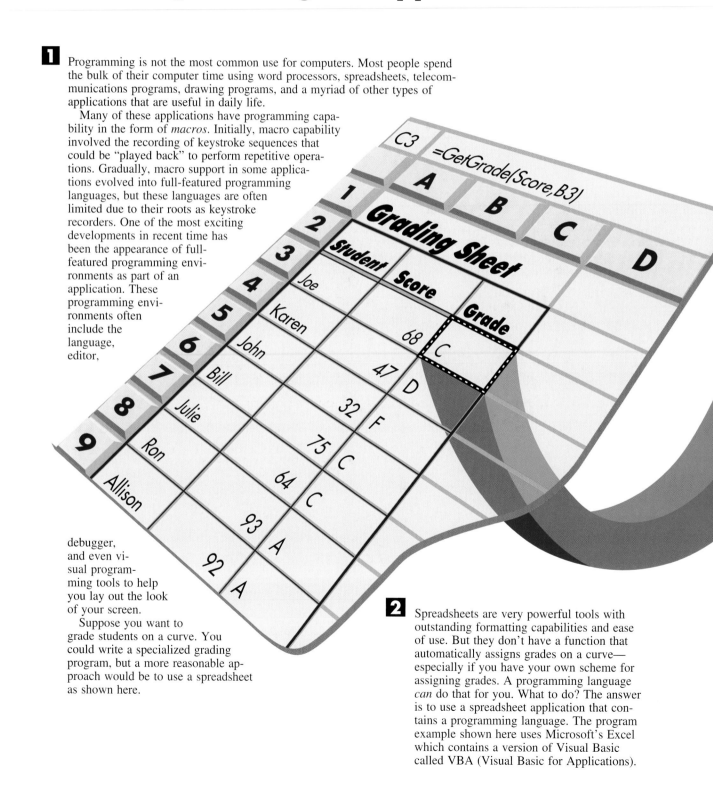

2 Spreadsheets are very powerful tools with outstanding formatting capabilities and ease of use. But they don't have a function that automatically assigns grades on a curve—especially if you have your own scheme for assigning grades. A programming language *can* do that for you. What to do? The answer is to use a spreadsheet application that contains a programming language. The program example shown here uses Microsoft's Excel which contains a version of Visual Basic called VBA (Visual Basic for Applications).

```
' This BASIC function works directly with the spreadsheet

Function GetGrade(r As Object, grade As Integer) As String
    ' BASIC initializes the following local variables to zero.
    ' C does not perform automatic initialization, so if this was
    ' C, Variable AverageVal would have to be set to zero manually.
    Dim cellnum As Integer
    Dim AverageVal As Double
    Dim MinVal As Integer
    Dim MaxVal As Integer
    Dim Ranking As Double
    MinVal = r.Cells(1) ' r.Cells(1) = First grade in the list
    MaxVal = r.Cells(1)
    ' Loop through all the grades in the list (r.Count)
    For cellnum = 1 To r.Count
        AverageVal = AverageVal + r.Cells(cellnum)  ' Add up the values of all cells
        ' Also search for the minimum and maximum value
        If r.Cells(cellnum) < MinVal Then MinVal = r.Cells(cellnum)
        If r.Cells(cellnum) > MaxVal Then MaxVal = r.Cells(cellnum)
    Next cellnum
    AverageVal = AverageVal / r.Count  ' Average = total/items
    ' If above average, scale it between average and max
    ' A different teacher might use a different algorithm to
    ' assign letter grades
    If grade > AverageVal Then
        Ranking = (grade - AverageVal) / (MaxVal - AverageVal)
    Else
        Ranking = -(AverageVal - grade) / (AverageVal - MinVal)
    End If
    ' The ranking is now -1 to 1 - let's scale it to -3 to 3
    Ranking = Ranking * 3
    ' The Select Case statements allows you to quickly compare
    ' variable Ranking with many different values.
    Select Case Ranking
        Case -3 to -2
            GetGrade = "F"
        Case -2 to -1
            GetGrade = "D"
        Case -1 To 1
            GetGrade = "C"
        Case 1 to 2
            GetGrade = "B"
        Case 2 to 3
            GetGrade = "A"
    End Select

End Function
```

3 Function GetGrade returns a letter grade that is calculated on a curve. The grades are weighted by first calculating the average, and then ranking each above-average grade between the average and the maximum and each below-average grade between the average and the minimum. The top two-thirds in the upper ranking are given A's and B's. The bottom two-thirds in the lower ranking are given F's and D's. Everyone else gets a C.

The function is called by placing the reference "=GetGrade(Score,Bn)" in each cell, where Score is a named range of all the scores for the class. (Think of Score as a variable that contains a list of numbers.) Bn identifies the cell that contains the grade to score and varies in this example from B3 to B9.

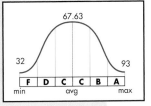

4 Many other applications provide opportunities for programming. Database applications have long had full-featured language capability, allowing programmers to create powerful custom database applications. Graphic programs have languages that let you manipulate images. Word processors have languages that allow rapid formatting of text, and sophisticated features such as word and sentence counting.

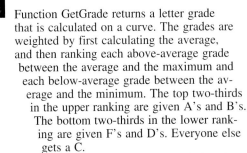

CHAPTER

29

How Event-Driven Programming Works

ONCE UPON A TIME, almost all programs were *linear*, beginning at a fixed point and then proceeding step by step to a fixed end. In the course of executing the program, input was requested from its user or perhaps from a file. Functions were called based on the input, and while the program might take varying paths during execution, the programmer could predict those paths. So long as the program ran, the only input it needed to process was the input it requested. This programming model worked reasonably well with text-oriented programs and with traditional operating systems, which provide functions to request user input. However, linear programming proved insufficient for use with modern graphical user interfaces (GUIs).

Unlike a text-based environment, in which your program must request information from the operating environment, a GUI environment constantly sends messages or calls functions in your program to indicate that some event has occurred. These events include anything from keystrokes to mouse movements, as well as notifications of changes to the environment itself—such as the movement of a window or a change in the color scheme. In this *event-driven environment*, your program must be prepared at all times to handle any of these events, or to disable events that you aren't prepared to handle.

Fortunately, event-driven environments provide features that help manage these various events. Most events have a default behavior that allows you in many cases to ignore any incoming information that you don't need. Event-driven environments also provide screen objects (also sometimes called components) that provide a "canned" functionality. For example, a graphical text input box routinely handles its own mouse and keyboard input. Your program can directly retrieve or set the value of the text at any time. Such objects make event-driven programming in many ways easier than traditional programming models, but the concept does take getting used to. This is especially true if you learned to program according to the linear programming model.

Event-Driven Programming

1 In a linear program that is not event driven, the user runs the program, which then proceeds to request information. The order in which the user enters data is entirely under the program's control, even if the program flow is not strictly linear. Software written for your city's building permit department might work in this manner.

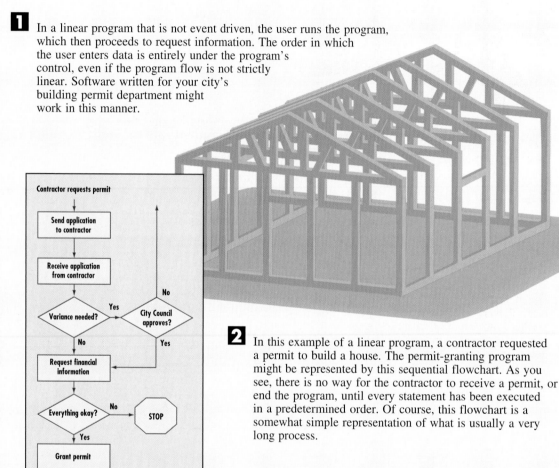

2 In this example of a linear program, a contractor requested a permit to build a house. The permit-granting program might be represented by this sequential flowchart. As you see, there is no way for the contractor to receive a permit, or end the program, until every statement has been executed in a predetermined order. Of course, this flowchart is a somewhat simple representation of what is usually a very long process.

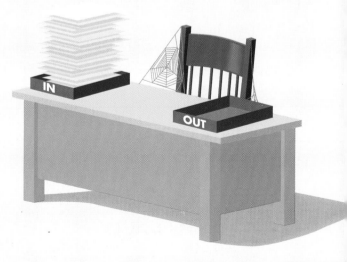

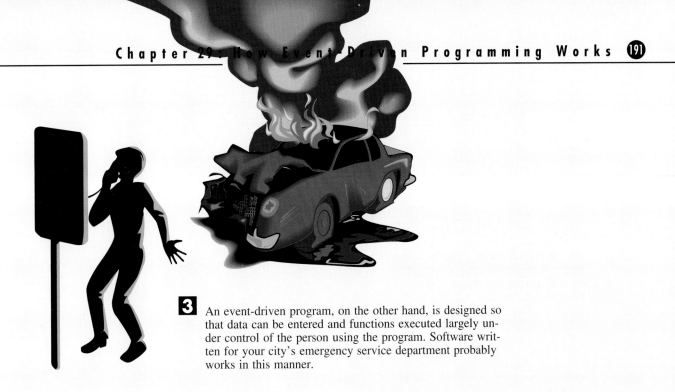

3 An event-driven program, on the other hand, is designed so that data can be entered and functions executed largely under control of the person using the program. Software written for your city's emergency service department probably works in this manner.

4 An event-driven program cannot be represented by a single sequential flowchart. Rather, you must use a series of smaller flowcharts that reflect responses to external events. Functions in the program can be triggered in any sequence, depending on these external events.

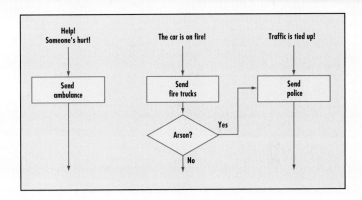

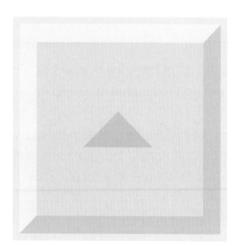

CHAPTER 30

How User Interface Design Works

WHEN YOU SIT down to use a program—whether a word processor, an accounting package, or a game—you don't see the effort that went into making the program. Nor do you see the code that makes it work. What you do see is the *user interface*: the part of the program that was written to interact with you, the user.

If you have designed a poor user interface, it won't matter how good your code is or how fast it runs. If, on the other hand, your interface is easy to use and learn, your program will probably be a success—even though it is not quite as fast or powerful as you might wish.

Major software developers carefully study user interfaces and work hard to create good ones. Custom versions of software, which can monitor what users actually do with it, help developers discover mistakes in the program or screen elements that are confusing. Some companies have user-interface design labs, where people are observed using the software.

As long as you are writing programs for your own use, user interface design is not a problem—it's always easy to use an interface that you created yourself. When you are writing code for others, however, one of the best approaches you can take in designing the user interface is to find a graphic designer to do it for you. As a programmer, you tend to be too close to your own work, and an outsider's perspective is essential. If this option is not available, be sure to test your interface on real users as early in the development process as possible.

Many programming environments now provide visual tools for creating your user interface. These tools allow you to draw objects on a screen, such as text boxes, list boxes, pictures, and text. This technique of laying out a program by drawing objects is often referred to as *visual programming*. The obvious advantage of these tools is that they speed up program development. Equally important is that they help you to rapidly prototype the appearance and behavior ("look and feel") of your program, and make it easy to revise the interface based on users' feedback.

Visual Programming

Creating a user interface in a graphical programming environment is as easy as drawing. The user interface is built from *screen objects* (also known as *controls*), each of which has its own appearance and characteristics.

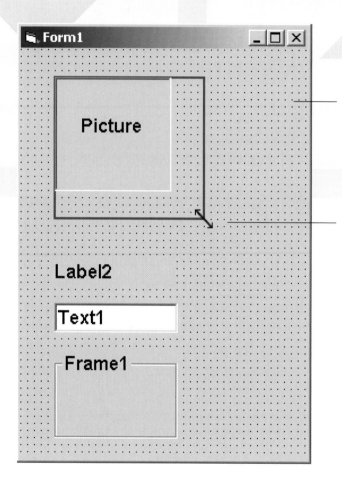

For those who don't find drawing easy, the screen area usually contains a grid that helps you align the controls you create. This grid is visible only while you are drawing the user interface; it does not appear when the program itself is running.

The size of a screen object can easily be changed, by clicking on a side or corner of the object and dragging the mouse. As you drag, a dotted or shaded line indicates the size the control will have when the mouse is released.

A user interface can be built from standard controls that are part of the programming language or operating system. Here you can see some of the controls that are available on most graphical operating systems.

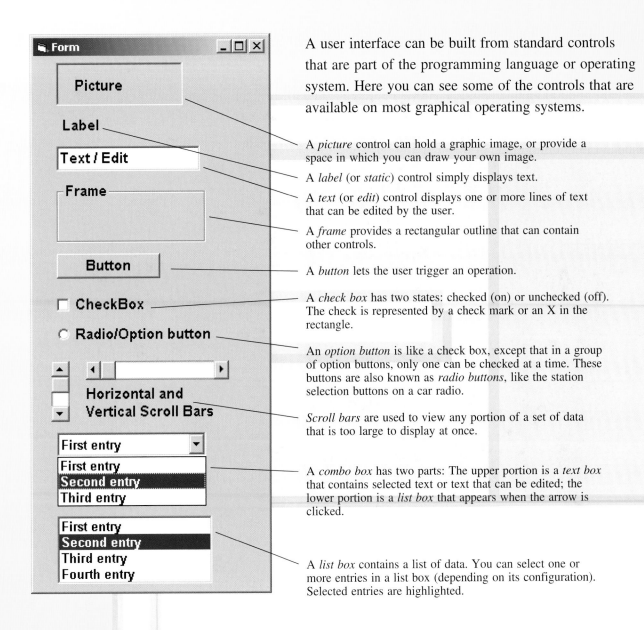

A *picture* control can hold a graphic image, or provide a space in which you can draw your own image.

A *label* (or *static*) control simply displays text.

A *text* (or *edit*) control displays one or more lines of text that can be edited by the user.

A *frame* provides a rectangular outline that can contain other controls.

A *button* lets the user trigger an operation.

A *check box* has two states: checked (on) or unchecked (off). The check is represented by a check mark or an X in the rectangle.

An *option button* is like a check box, except that in a group of option buttons, only one can be checked at a time. These buttons are also known as *radio buttons*, like the station selection buttons on a car radio.

Scroll bars are used to view any portion of a set of data that is too large to display at once.

A *combo box* has two parts: The upper portion is a *text box* that contains selected text or text that can be edited; the lower portion is a *list box* that appears when the arrow is clicked.

A *list box* contains a list of data. You can select one or more entries in a list box (depending on its configuration). Selected entries are highlighted.

Each of these controls can be manipulated by the code in your program. When a user performs an operation on a control—such as clicking a button or entering text—the control will call functions in your program that tell your program what event has occurred. Their function-calling ability makes controls ideal for creating event-driven programs.

Look and Feel

The Wrong Way

It's very tempting to try and give your application a unique look to help it stand out. But it's best to have your application follow the standards of the environment for which you are programming. Otherwise, your users must learn and remember features specific only to your application.

Toolbars are fine, but never rely on toolbar buttons alone to convey information. A symbol that is obvious to you may confuse someone else. Be sure that any operation that can be triggered by a toolbar button can also be triggered by a menu or other method.

Different fonts and colors without meaning are a distraction.

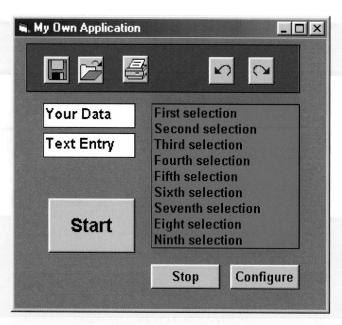

If you must use color, let the users customize the colors to suit their own tastes. You may love blue on red, but others may hate it—or worse yet, may be color blind and oblivious to all your hard work. Keep in mind that your program may end up running on a black and white monitor on which different colors might look identical.

Avoid inconsistent 3-D effects and fancy text. Is there a good reason for one button to be larger than another?

The Right Way

This user interface is a dramatic improvement over the one on the left.

A standard menu bar should contain commands that duplicate the functions on the toolbar. Most people interpret text faster than images.

This toolbar is similar to those used in many applications. The File button is placed at the left, and other command buttons are logically grouped. The 3-D raised effect invites the user to click the buttons.

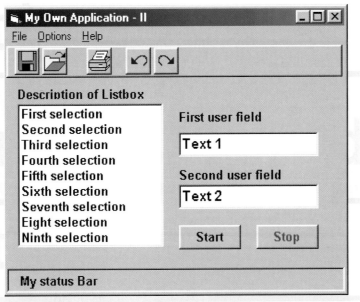

The list boxes and text controls have a white background; white is used consistently in this form to indicate places where the user can select or enter data. Each control that can accept user input has a label attached that describes the control. One letter in each menu item is underlined, making it possible to jump directly to the control for that label using the keyboard. In most cases you will want your program to work with the keyboard as well as the mouse.

An inset status bar displays information about whatever control is pointed to or selected.

Buttons have a consistent size and shape. The use of color for the Stop! button makes sense because it draws the user to that button—important, since this program needs to make the button easy to find quickly. The choice of red, typically associated with "stop" or "danger," is appropriate. A Start or Go button might use green.

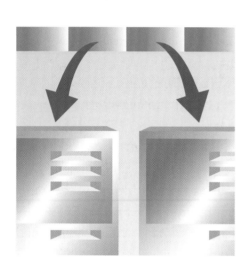

How Object-Oriented, Component, and Client-Server Programming Works

ONE OF THE most exciting changes in software development over the past decade has been the rise of *object-oriented programming* (OOP) techniques. You have already seen that a large part of programming consists of managing the complexity of variables and code. Variables are organized into groups and data structures. Code is divided into clearly named functions that are grouped into related modules.

Object-oriented programming makes it easier for a programmer to both reduce complexity and create reusable code modules. The most important characteristic of OOP is the ability to associate code tightly with a particular data structure, and to hide the variables in that structure so that they can only be accessed by using the functions that belong to that structure.

Consider a music collection that contains records, compact discs, and tapes. Each album might be represented by a structure containing the name, category, and publisher of the album. With OOP, each album can also contain a function to retrieve the name of the album. For example, if you had a variable of type Album called Album1, you might access the Name variable using Album1.Name, and call the GetAlbumName function using Album1.GetAlbumName(). You can set up the structure so that the Name variable is initialized when the structure is created, and is then hidden from the rest of the program. Other functions must use the GetAlbumName() function to determine the name of the album.

This technique has several advantages. First, since the rest of the program has no access to the Name variable, you don't have to worry about some other function accidentally changing the name of an album. Next, by hiding the Name variable, you have once again reduced the complexity of the program by reducing the number of variables that you need to track.

But the benefits don't stop there. OOP provides a capability called *overloading*, which allows a function name to be reused. Let's say you want to manage a stamp collection in the same program with the music collection. This stamp collection could use a structure called StampAlbum with its own variables, including one called Name that would contain the name of the stamp album. This structure could then have its own GetAlbumName() function. The type of structure you are using tells the language which of the GetAlbumName functions to call. So instead of tracking separate variables or functions for each type of object, you only need to re-member that the GetAlbumName function retrieves the name of an object.

OOP technology, when used correctly, can save you an enormous amount of time and effort—but OOP does take time to learn to use effectively. The C++ language (pronounced "See-Plus-Plus") is currently the most popular object-oriented language and is readily available on all major computer systems and environments, though most other modern languages support object oriented programming as well. Java, in particular has strong object oriented features.

And this is just the beginning. Because once you get used to the idea of building a program from objects, you can't help but ask some interesting questions. What if you could buy pieces of of an application that contain all the code for handling an object, instead of writing it from scratch? And what if you could create a program out of objects, where instead of running on a single machine, the objects were running on different machines connected by a network?

The answers to those questions, as you will soon see, have brought about changes in computer programming that are nothing short of revolutionary.

Working with Objects

Consider a music collection that consists of compact discs, cassette tapes, and vinyl records. All three of these types of musical album share certain characteristics. In an object-oriented language, you can create a type of structure to represent these common traits. Structures in object-oriented languages are often called *classes*.

1 The class named Album is a data structure that contains variables for the name of the album, the category, and the publisher. Object-oriented programming (OOP) languages allow you to create functions that belong to a class. In this case, function GetAlbumName() returns the value of the Album_Name variable. In C++, class Album could be defined thus:

Class Album

Album_Name

Category

Publisher

Function GetAlbumName( )
Virtual Function Play(SongNumber)

```
class Album {
    // These are private variables - they can only
    // be accessed by functions that belong to the class.
    char *Album_Name;
    char *Category;
    char *Publisher;
public:
    // These are public functions - they can be called
    // from anywhere in the program.
    char *GetAlbumName();
    // The keyword virtual will be explained later.
    virtual int Play(int SongNumber);
};
```

The *public:* command in this listing is a C++ command that declares that the following functions can be called from anywhere in the program. You can also declare private functions that can only be called by other functions in the class.

2 If you create a variable of type Album called FirstAlbum, you can access Album_Name in that variable using FirstAlbum.Album_Name. But you could only use this within a class function because it is a *private* variable, hidden to the rest of your program. The function GetAlbumName, however, is *public* and can be called from anywhere in the program, using FirstAlbum.GetAlbumName().

3 OOP languages provide a feature called *inheritance*, in which a new class inherits the variables and functions of another class. In this case, we create three new classes to represent compact discs, tapes, and records. In reality, you would never create a variable of class Album, since a real album must take one of these forms. However, the existence of this class allows us to declare variables and functions that can be shared by other classes, reducing the amount of programming required.

Because class CD is a descendant of class Album, you can call the function GetAlbumName() for this class even if you do not write a new GetAlbumName() function. The language will automatically use the function defined for the Album class.

Each of these classes has its own variable that is unique to its type: A CD has a serial number, a tape may be recorded with Dolby, and a record has an associated playing speed. Each class can also have additional private functions of its own. Because CDs, tapes and records work differently, each class needs its own Play function. The Tape class Play function needs to know how to reverse the tape if necessary. The Record class may need to indicate that the record must be flipped to play a certain song. Class Tape might be defined in C++ as follows:

Class CD

Album_Name

Category

Publisher

Function GetAlbumName( )
Virtual Function Play(SongNumber)

SerialNumber

Public:
Function GetSerialNumber( )
Function Play(SongNumber)

Class Tape

Album_Name

Category

Publisher

Function GetAlbumName( )
Virtual Function Play(SongNumber)

Dolby

Public:
Function GetDolby( )
Function Play(SongNumber)

Class Record

Album_Name

Category

Publisher

Function GetAlbumName( )
Virtual Function Play(SongNumber)

Speed

Public:
Function GetSpeed( )
Function Play(SongNumber)

```
class Tape: public Album {
    // Class tape inherits all public variables and functions
    // belonging to class Album.
    char *Dolby;
    // Reverse is a private function - it can only
    // be called by functions that belong to this class.
    int Reverse();
public:
    char *GetDolby();
    int Play(int SongNumber);
}
```

4 A real music collection might contain a mix of records, CDs, and tapes. C++ allows you to represent this collection by an array, where each entry in the array is a pointer to an object of class Album. These pointers can point to an object that belongs to the CD, Record, or Tape class. This makes it easy to mix the types of albums that are pointed to by the array. Such an array is created using this declaration:

```
Album *AlbumList[ARRAYLENGTH]; // ARRAYLENGTH is the size of the array
```

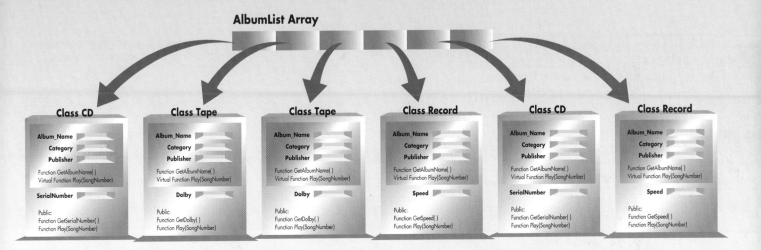

AlbumList Array

| Class CD | Class Tape | Class Tape | Class Record | Class CD | Class Record |

5 It's easy to determine the name of any album using this technique. For example, to obtain the name of the third album in your collection, you would call AlbumList[3]->GetAlbumName().

But what if you want to play a particular song? Each album type has to have its own Play function because of the unique requirements of the class. How does the language know whether to call the CD Play function, or that of the Tape or Record class?

The original definition of class Album contained a declaration for a Play function that includes the *virtual* keyword. This is an instruction to C++ to add hidden code to provide special handling for this function. When the program is run, it will automatically determine which object class is being referenced and call the correct Play function for that object. Thus, in this example, the function AlbumList[4]->Play(3) calls the Play function for the CD class, not the Album class.

Software Components and Distributed Computing

No true music collection is ever complete, and HCW Record company is there to help you build your collection. Their programmers have done a lot of work to make sure that your phone order is processed efficiently. Here's how they did it...

Send 1 Compurock CD
2580 Main Street
Generic Town, Calif. 95896
$15.96 + 8.25% Tax
Visa 4123 4567 8901 2345
Exp. 02/09

HCW Records, may I take your order?

The people who wrote the order entry program didn't have to write all of its objects. They were able to purchase standalone software components to perform a variety of tasks. The functions in these components can be called as if they were part of the main program. The different components can even be written in different languages.

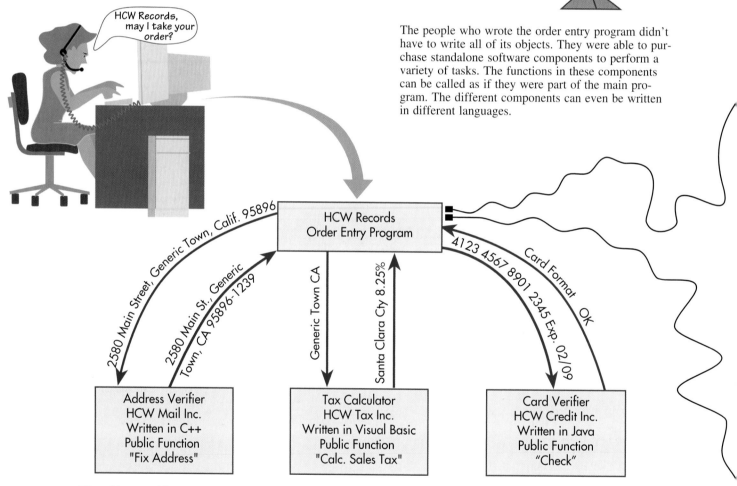

HCW Records
Order Entry Program

2580 Main Street, Generic Town, Calif. 95896

2580 Main St., Generic Town, CA 95896-1239

Generic Town CA

Santa Clara Cty 8.25%

4123 4567 8901 2345 Exp. 02/09

Card Format OK

Address Verifier
HCW Mail Inc.
Written in C++
Public Function
"Fix Address"

Tax Calculator
HCW Tax Inc.
Written in Visual Basic
Public Function
"Calc. Sales Tax"

Card Verifier
HCW Credit Inc.
Written in Java
Public Function
"Check"

The address verifier component takes an address in any format, and changes it to match post office specifications. This one changes the word "street" to the abbreviated "St.", "Calif" to the standard abbreviation "CA", and adds the Zip+4 zip code.

The tax calculator component looks up the city and finds out what county it is in, then returns the correct tax rate for that county.

Every credit card number has to follow certain rules such as the number of digits and sum of digits. This component checks to see if the card number is valid according to those rules and returns a "good card" or "bad card" result to the main program.

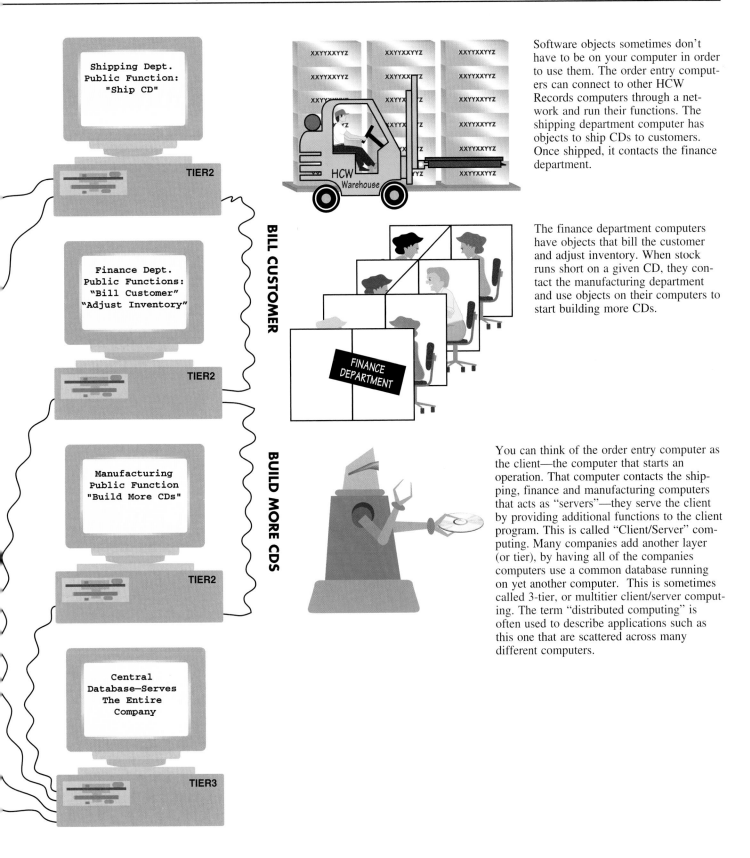

**Shipping Dept.
Public Function:
"Ship CD"**

TIER2

**Finance Dept.
Public Functions:
"Bill Customer"
"Adjust Inventory"**

TIER2

**Manufacturing
Public Function
"Build More CDs"**

TIER2

**Central
Database—Serves
The Entire
Company**

TIER3

BILL CUSTOMER

BUILD MORE CDS

HCW
Warehouse

FINANCE
DEPARTMENT

Software objects sometimes don't have to be on your computer in order to use them. The order entry computers can connect to other HCW Records computers through a network and run their functions. The shipping department computer has objects to ship CDs to customers. Once shipped, it contacts the finance department.

The finance department computers have objects that bill the customer and adjust inventory. When stock runs short on a given CD, they contact the manufacturing department and use objects on their computers to start building more CDs.

You can think of the order entry computer as the client—the computer that starts an operation. That computer contacts the shipping, finance and manufacturing computers that acts as "servers"—they serve the client by providing additional functions to the client program. This is called "Client/Server" computing. Many companies add another layer (or tier), by having all of the companies computers use a common database running on yet another computer. This is sometimes called 3-tier, or multitier client/server computing. The term "distributed computing" is often used to describe applications such as this one that are scattered across many different computers.

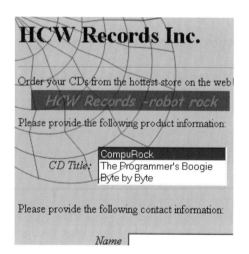

How Internet Programming Works

I N THE LAST chapter you saw how large companies can use distributed computing to create programs that run on several computers at once. But while corporations are gradually shifting to distributed computing, there is one group that has adopted it to such a degree that they routinely run applications that are made up of many different objects, written in different languages, that may be scattered across dozens of computers around the world.

And chances are good that you are part of that group. Because the greatest use today of distributed computing are by those who use the Internet.

Consider what happens on your computer when you browse the world wide web. The first thing that happens is that you run a program called a web browser. The web browser requests web pages from other computers on the Internet and receives pages in a format called HTML. HTML stands for "HyperText Markup Language".

Language? That's right—HTML is a language designed to display text and graphics. It includes instructions for formatting text, and retrieving additional graphics or objects from the Internet. HTML is an interpreted language (see chapter 23 for a reminder on the difference between compilers and interpreters)—and the program that interprets HTML is the web browser itself. In other words: much of a web browser is really nothing more than an HTML interpreter.

HTML is fine for formatting text, but it's not very capable when it comes to interacting with the user or performing complex operations or calculations. Fortunately, modern web browsers aren't limited to interpreting HTML. They can also interpret a language called JavaScript, which is actually a bit closer to the C language than it's Java namesake. Microsoft's Internet Explorer can, in addition to Javascript, also interpret a language called VB Script which is based on Visual Basic. In each case, these languages allow the browser to run fairly sophisticated Internet based programs.

The web browser runs on your computer and interprets the HTML and scripting code in the web pages it receives from the Internet—but where do those pages come from? They come from other computers that are running a program called a "web server". A web server receives requests from browser and sends back web pages.

It probably won't surprise you at this point to learn that the web server can also act as an interpreter. Different web servers have different capabilities, but all of them have at least the ability to run other programs and use the results to create a web page. Those programs can be written in virtually any language (C++, Java, Visual Basic and Perl are popular choices). Some web servers can directly interpret languages such as Java or Visual Basic as well. This allows web servers to perform complex operations ranging from creating maps for a given location, to trading stocks, to allowing you to purchase compact discs over the Internet.

Most programmers still start out by learning to write simple programs that run on a single computer, but there is little doubt that web programming is the wave of the future, and will become an important skill for every programmer.

How Internet Programming Works

HCW Records, like many companies, has opened its own online store for buying music through the world wide web. As web programmers, their software uses new languages such as HTML and Javascript, and continues to be distributed across many computers. Now the client computer is the customer—running their own web browser.

Here's part of the HTML code for this page as it looks on the web server before it is sent out to the client customer's web browser.:

```
<html>
<head>
<META name=VI60_defaultClientScript content=JavaScript>
<meta HTTP-EQUIV="Content-Type" CONTENT="text/html; charset=windows-1252">
<meta HTTP-EQUIV="Content-Language" CONTENT="en-us">
<title>HCW Purchase Page</title>

<SCRIPT ID=clientEventHandlersJS LANGUAGE=javascript>
<!--

function Rnd256(){
  return(Math.random() * 128 + 127);
}

function window_onload() {
  document.bgColor=  Math.floor((Rnd256() << 16) + (Rnd256() <<8) + Rnd256());
}

//-->
</SCRIPT>
<SCRIPT LANGUAGE=javascript FOR=window EVENT=onload>
<!--
  window_onload()
//-->
</SCRIPT>
</head>

<h1>HCW Records Inc.</h1>
<hr>
<p>Order your CDs from the hottest store on the web!</p>
<p><img border="0" src="www.hcwrecords.com/ourlogo.gif" width="276" height="90"></p>
<p> </p>
<form METHOD="POST" ACTION="www.hcwrecords.com/orders.cgi">
  <p>Please provide the following product information:</p>
  <blockquote>
    <table>
      <tr>
        <td ALIGN="right"><em>CD Title:</em></td>
        <td><select NAME="Product_ProductName" size="3">
            <option SELECTED>CompuRock
            <option>The Programmer's Boogie
            <option>Byte by Byte
            </select></td>
      </tr>
    </table>

  [. . . additional input fields . . .]

  <p>Enter your Credit Card number and expiration date in the space provided
  below.</p>
  <blockquote>
    <p><input TYPE="TEXT" NAME="CreditCardNumber" SIZE="50" MAXLENGTH="50"><br>
    </p>
  </blockquote>
  <input TYPE="submit" VALUE="Send Order" name="Send">
</form>
<hr>
<h5>HWC Records Inc.<br>
Copyright © 2000, HCW Records - All rights reserved.<br>
Revised: <!--webbot bot="TimeStamp" S-Type="EDITED" S-Format="%B %d, %Y" -->
</h5>

</html>
```

HCW Records Inc.

Order your CDs from the hottest store on the web!

HCW Records -robot rock

Please provide the following product information:

CD Title: CompuRock / The Programmer's Boogie / Byte by Byte

Please provide the following contact information:

Name
Street Address
Address (cont.)
City
State/Province
Zip/Postal Code
Country
E-mail

Enter your Credit Card number and expiration date in the space provided below.

Send Order

HWC Records Inc.
Copyright © 2000, HCW Records - All rights reserved.
Revised: February 06, 2000

Meta tags provide information that some browsers can use, such as the language of the page or keywords for search engines.

The title will show up in the caption bar for some browsers.

The <!-- symbol indicates a comment in the HTML language. Older browsers will ignore these comments, but newer ones read them to see if there are instructions in languages other than HTML. The <Script> tag tells the browser that what follows is no longer HTML but, in this case, Javascript. That's right—we're switching programming languages in the middle of the page!

The Rnd256 function simply returns a number between 128 and 255

The window_onload() function sets the background color of the page to a random color, where the red, green and blue parts of the color are each a random number from 128 to 255.

The code instructs the browser to call the window_onload() function every time the browser loads the page.

The img tag tells the browser to load an image—the image can be anywhere on the Internet.

The form tag tells the browser that a form containing fields that can be edited by the user follows. The information in the fields will be sent to the Internet location specified, in this case "www.hcwrecords.com/orders.cgi". This is the name of the program or object that will be run on the web server when the user submits the form.

A Select input type defines a list box from which you can choose options.

The <!-- symbol again represents a comment, but in this case the comment will be read by the web server before the page is sent to the user. The web server program will interpret the command—in this case a command to send to the user the date and time on which the web page was last edited.

As you can see, a web page can contain HTML code, Script code to be run by the web browser, and script code to run on the server before the page is sent out.

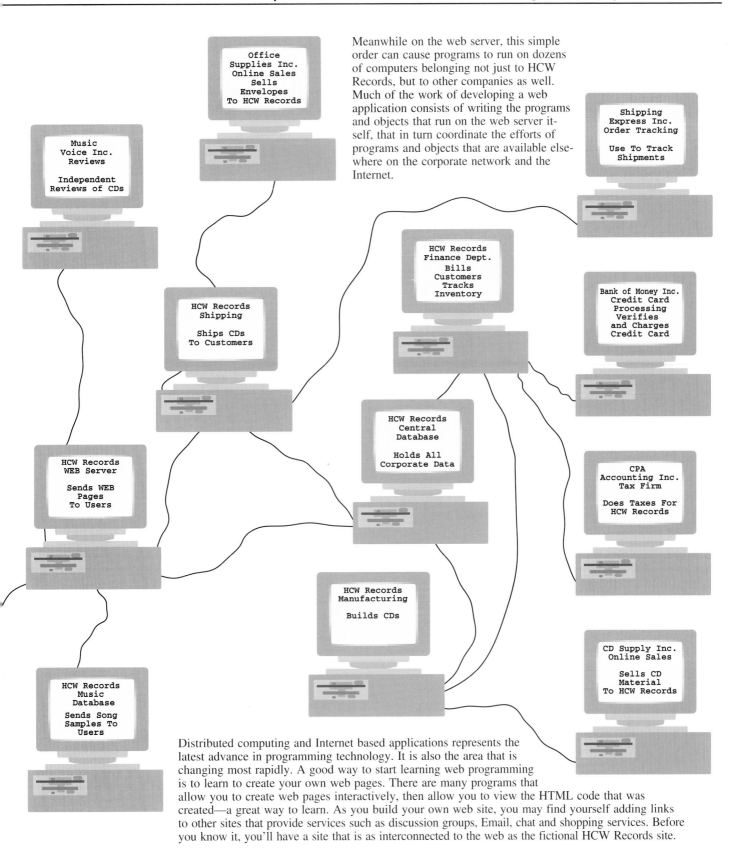

Meanwhile on the web server, this simple order can cause programs to run on dozens of computers belonging not just to HCW Records, but to other companies as well. Much of the work of developing a web application consists of writing the programs and objects that run on the web server itself, that in turn coordinate the efforts of programs and objects that are available elsewhere on the corporate network and the Internet.

Distributed computing and Internet based applications represents the latest advance in programming technology. It is also the area that is changing most rapidly. A good way to start learning web programming is to learn to create your own web pages. There are many programs that allow you to create web pages interactively, then allow you to view the HTML code that was created—a great way to learn. As you build your own web site, you may find yourself adding links to other sites that provide services such as discussion groups, Email, chat and shopping services. Before you know it, you'll have a site that is as interconnected to the web as the fictional HCW Records site.

CHAPTER 33

How Embedded Programming Works, and How to Program Your VCR

WHEN YOU HEAR the word *computer*, you probably think of a keyboard, screen, disk drive, mouse…the classic desktop machine. But you should also think of your microwave oven, automobile, telephone, television, and—perhaps most of all—video cassette recorder.

All of these machines are controlled in one form or another by a computer, usually a small 8-bit or 16-bit microprocessor. Just as your computer has an operating system that controls the disk, screen, and keyboard, so do these machines contain very small operating systems that make them work. Your VCR's operating system could not possibly run a disk drive, but it knows how to rewind a tape. It does not read a keyboard, but it can detect that you've pressed the Play button on the front panel, and it can interpret the infrared pulses that come from your remote control.

And just as your computer can be programmed using languages such as BASIC and C, so, too, can your VCR be programmed.

Before you panic at the thought, rest assured that your VCR has an extremely simple programming language, designed to be used by nonprogrammers, even those who haven't read this book! And now that you know how programming works, what once may have seemed complex will be easy to comprehend.

That said, the first step is to figure out the language of your particular VCR….

Programming a VCR

The first step in writing any program is figuring out how to do the task manually. Suppose you want to record a one-hour show that runs on channel 5 from 8:00 p.m. to 9:00 p.m. on Saturday. To do it manually, you would

- Wait until Saturday at 8:00 p.m.
- Set the VCR to channel 5.
- Press the Record button on your VCR.
- Wait until 9:00 p.m.
- Press the stop button on your VCR.

Now all you need to do is convert these five steps into a program that your VCR can execute to record the program you want. Most modern VCRs display the programming information on the TV screen, though some older machines use a display on their front panel.

▲ Tell Your VCR That You Want to Create a Program

Somewhere on your VCR or remote control you'll find a button that tells your VCR that you want to program it to record a show. It might be called something like Prog or Program or Timer. You may need to search your VCR manual to find this button—but rest assured, if your VCR is programmable, there is such a command.

Once you enter the programming mode, some VCRs will ask if you want to create a program or set the clock. Others may go directly into the next step.

Tell Your VCR Which Program You Are Creating ▶

Most VCRs let you record more than one program. Before you start a program, you need to choose which one you are setting. In this example, the VCR lets you choose among four options, by pressing one of the numbers 1 through 4 on the remote control.

Set the Start Time, Stop Time, and Channel ▶

The main programming screen is where you create the program itself. In most cases, you'll see a flashing square on the screen where you can enter numbers using your remote control. There will also be a Clear or Reset key that allows you to "backspace" to correct mistakes. Simply "type" in the date, start time, stop time, and channel number to fill the blanks on the screen.

Some VCRs also allow you to program the machine to record every day at the same time, or once a week at a particular day and time.

◀ Tell the VCR to Execute the Program

Your VCR may now display a summary of the program that you created, and any other programs that you had already created. Now you need to tell the VCR that you are finished programming. On some VCRs, you press the Program or Timer key again to get out of programming mode. Then you can use your VCR normally.

Once you have programmed the VCR and want it to start waiting for your show, you will need to tell the VCR to execute the program. This step varies from VCR to VCR. Sometimes you simply insert a tape cassette and turn the machine off, and the VCR will automatically start the program and turn itself on to record at 8:00 p.m. Saturday. On other VCRs you press a special Timer button to turn on the program.

That's all there is to it. Just as languages differ, VCR programming will vary from machine to machine. But once you understand the fundamentals of what commands *must* be present for a programmable VCR to work, it is simply a matter of finding the way those commands are implemented for your particular VCR.

And now that you understand the features that are present in most computer languages, you will find that learning a particular language is simply a matter of figuring out how that language implements those features.

Where Do You Go From Here?

When you learned how to read, you did not start by reading entire words. First you learned the alphabet, and the sounds that each letter makes. Next you learned how the letters combined to form words and finally, how to combine words to communicate an idea.

Computer programming is similar. This book describes the "alphabet" of programming—the fundamental ideas that you will find in any computer language. No one language was taught in detail, though you did see examples in C++ and BASIC, two of the most commonly used languages.

If all you wanted to do was find out a little bit about what computer programming is all about, you can stop here. However, if you are interested in learning more and writing your own programs, you should find learning a specific language a much easier process than it would have been without this book.

There are dozens of books available that cover particular language implementations for beginners. Your best bet is to explore your local bookstore, or a good technical bookstore if you have one nearby, and choose one that strikes you as easy to read and understand. Most local and community colleges also offer courses on programming, as do many private vocational schools.

As you have seen, there is a lot more to programming than stringing code together. Learning to design software, define complex data structures, and use and create new algorithms are often considered the most exciting aspects of the art of programming. In fact, when you arrive at this level of programming, the term *computer science* is more appropriate.

The good news is *How Computer Programming Works* did not limit itself to programming alone. We covered many of the subjects that a computer science student needs to learn, though obviously not in great detail. To learn more about these, see if you can find a high school or introductory level computer science text at a good technical bookstore or a college bookstore. Many colleges and universities offer programs and extension classes in computer science as well.

But when all is said and done, there is ultimately one technique that every programmer uses that is more valuable than any book or any class. Get a copy of the language of your choice (preferably BASIC for absolute beginners, C++ for those who plan to go beyond the hobbyist stage), install it on your computer and start working through the examples provided with the language manuals.

Then, just start writing your own programs. Don't be afraid to experiment and make mistakes (you will make a lot of mistakes—we all do). You will find yourself programming sooner than you thought possible, and having a lot of fun in the process.

! = operator, 57

& operator, 57

&& operator, 57

( ) (parentheses), 56

* operator, 56

/ operator, 56

: separator, 53

: = operator, 53

; separator, 53, 181

<<>> operator, 57

<==> operator, 57

< > operator, 57

= operator, 53, 56–57

= = operator, 53, 57

^ operator, 56–57

{ } (braces), 59, 181

| operator, 57

|| operator, 57

A

accumulator, 173

ADA, 156

addition, 57

addition operator (+), 53

address, variable, 21–25

address register, 174

alarm system example, 38–41

Algol, 156

algorithms, 105–143, 159

AND operation, 37–38, 43, 57

APL, 157

append strings, 54

applications programming, 186–187

arrays, 75, 77–78, 80–81

   implementing queues in, 92

   implementing stacks in, 91

   one-based, 109, 112

   one-dimensional, 78

   scanning, 109

   two-dimensional, 78

   zero-based, 109–110

array of structures, 83

array variables, 77

ASCII code, 31–34

assembler, 14, 173, 176

assembly language, 11, 173–174, 176–177

   code, 14–15

   evolution of, 157

assigning variables, 53, 56

assignment operators, 53, 56

B

BASIC, 153, 157, 183–187

begin statement, 59

binary files, 127

binary search, 116, 118–119

binary search trees, 101–103

binary trees, 101–103

BIOS, 5

BitBlt, 133

bitmapped (rasterized) image, 133

bits, 9, 28, 43

blocks of code, 51, 59–61

boiling water example, 60–61

Boolean algebra, 37

Boolean operators, 57

Boolean truth tables, 37–39

Boolean variables, 37–43

boundary condition, 109

braces, 59, 181

bubble sort algorithm, 121–123

bugs, 167

buttons, 195, 197

C

C++, 154, 156, 199–200, 202–203

card deck example, 77–78, 80–81

case conversion program, 181, 184–185

central processing unit (CPU), 9, 173

character pointers, 181

character sets, 31–35

check boxes, 195

children (tree branches), 101

chores example, 90–91

C language, 15, 154, 156, 179–181

class browsers, 165

classes, 83, 202

client/server programming, 205

closing a file, 128, 131

COBOL, 157

code, 49–71

code blocks, 51, 59–61

code pages, 35

coding (program), 164–165

coding standards, 165

combo boxes, 195

commands, programming, 107

compact-disk collection example, 83–84, 86–87, 96

comparison operators, 57

comparisons, 57, 63, 65

compilers, 14, 149–151, 164

complement, 57

component software, 204–205

computer science, 209

constant variable, 21

constructing a program, phases of, 146–147

control characters, ASCII codes for, 33

control frame, 195

controls, designing, 194–195

coordinate systems, for drawing, 138–139

counter variable, 63

CPU, 9, 173

CRLF pair, 127

cross-reference programs, 165

currency variables, 24

D

database applications, 121, 187

data manipulation, 19

data register, 173

data structures. *See* structures

debuggers, 180

debugging, 60, 159–160, 166–167

decision trees, 101–103

deck of cards example, 77–78, 80–81

declaring variables, 21, 67–68, 70–71

deleting data from a file, 130

design process (programs), 159–160, 162–163

dice-rolling simulator, 141–143

dimensioning variables, 67

direct access of a variable, 47

disk drives, 8

distributed computing, 205, 211

divide and conquer, 116

division, 56

documentation (program), 159, 164–165

double indirection, 46

double linked lists, 95, 99

drawing, 138–139

drawing grid, 194

drawing programs, 136

drives, disk and tape, 8

dynamic variables, 67

EBCDIC code, 31–32

edit control, 195

editor (program), 164

embedded programming, 213–215

emergency-services program, 191

encryption, 32

end statement, 59

equivalence, 57

error checking, runtime, 180

event-driven environments, 189

event-driven programming, 189–191

Excel, 186

executable file, 165, 177

execution of code, 51

exponentiation, 56

F

factorial, 115

FALSE Boolean value, 37, 39

FIFO (first in first out) queue, 89

file functions, libraries of, 127

file operations, 129–130

files

  closing, 128, 131

  deleting data from, 130

  input and output, 128

  inserting data into, 130

  loading and saving, 127

  opening, 128, 130

  searching, 128

finding. *See* searching

fixed-length records, 131

flag bits, 41

flag register, 173

flags, 37–43

flight simulators, 141

flowcharts, 63, 65, 162, 190–191

flow (program), 6–9, 51, 63–65, 162, 190–191

For...Next loops, 63, 65, 81, 109, 113, 115

For statements, 63

Forth, 157

Fortran, 156

frame, control, 195

full-featured programming environments, 186

function libraries, 165, 179

  file functions, 127

  graphics functions, 134

function overloading, 199

function parameters, 68

functions, 51, 59–61, 81

  that call themselves, 90

  file, 127

  hierarchy of, 60

  image, 133

  recursive, 115

  reentrant, 90

function variables on the stack, 90

G

general purpose register, 173

global variables, 67

GOTO statements in BASIC, 184

grading program, 186–187

graphical user interfaces (GUIs), 189, 193–197

graphics, 133–134, 136–139

graphics algorithms, 136–137

graphics function libraries, 134

graphics objects, rasterized, 137

graphics primitives, 133

grid, drawing, 194

grouping statements, 59

GUI environments, 189, 193–197

H

hardware, 5–9

hex (hexadecimal), 15, 42–43, 177

hierarchy of functions, 60

high-level languages, 11, 14, 179

HTML, 207–210

Hypertext Markup Language, 207, 210

I

If...Then statements, 63

image functions, 133

implementing a computer language, 149

incremental compilation, 149

incrementing a pointer, 181

index file, 131

indirection, 46–47, 95

inheritance, in C++, 202

input processing, 8

inputting to a file, 128–130

instruction pointer (IP), 174

integers, 27

  converting to and from strings, 35

  used as counters, 63

Internet programming, 210

interpreters, 14, 149–151, 164

I/O (Input/Output), 9

J

Java, 156
Javascript, 207, 210

K

keystroke macros, 186

L

label (or static) control, 195
languages (computer), 11, 149–151, 153–154
   choosing, 153
   evolution of, 156–157
   hierarchy of, 14–15
   high-level, 179
   low-level, 179
lawn mowing example, 64–65
librarian (library program), 165
libraries of functions, 165, 179
   graphics functions, 134
   file functions, 127
lifetime of a variable, 70
LIFO (last in first out) queue, 89
linear programs, 189–190
linked lists, 95–96, 98–99
linker, 164
Lisp, 157
list boxes, 195
listing programs, 165
lists, linked, 95–96, 98–99
LOGO language, 12–13, 157
loops (program), 63, 65, 81, 109, 113, 115
lowercase, converting, 181, 184–185
low-level languages, 11, 179

M

machine code, 164, 176
machine language, 9, 15
macros, 186
mailboxes example, 22–25
masks, 43
mask variable, 43
maximum value, finding, 113
memory management, 51, 95
menu bar, 197
microcode, 176
minimum value, finding, 113
Modula2, 156
monitor program, 5
Monte Carlo method, 141–143
morphing algorithm, 136
mowing the lawn example, 64–65
multiplication, 56
multitier programming, 205
Murphy's law of programming, 167
music collection example, 199–200, 202–203

N

names of variables, 22–23
naming structures, 84
negation, 56
networks, 205, 210–211
node (binary tree), 102
node value (binary tree), 103
NOT operation, 37, 39, 57
NULL character, 35

numbers, 27–29

  categories of, 27

  string representation of, 34

numeric types, 27–29, 54

numeric variables, 27–29, 54

O

object file, 164–165

object inheritance, 202

object-oriented programming (OOP), 84, 153, 199–200, 202–203

objects, 83, 202–205

one-based arrays, 109, 112

one-dimensional arrays, 78

opening a file, 128, 130

operating systems, use of linked lists, 95

operators, 53–54, 56–57

option buttons, 195

organizing data, 73–103

OR operation, 37–38, 43, 57

output processing, 9, 128

overloading a function, 199

P

pages, code, 35

paint programs, 137

parameter passing, 68, 70–71

parameters, 59, 68

parentheses, 56

Pascal, 153, 156

passing by reference (parameters), 68, 70

passing by value (parameters), 68, 71

P-Code, 149

Perl, 207

permit-granting program, 190

picket fence problem, 110, 112–113

picture control, 195

pixels, 133

pointers, 45–47

  character, 181

  incrementing, 181

  linking structures, 98–99

  uninitialized, 180

  wrapping, 92

popping data from the stack, 89–90

private variables, 202

procedure, 59

profiler, 165

program blocks, 51, 59–61

program code, 49–71

program flow. *See* flowcharts; flow (program)

programming, 5

Prolog, 157

prototyping, 163

pseudocode, 63, 162

public variables, 202

pushing data onto the stack, 89–90

Q

queues, 89, 92–93

quick sort algorithm, 121, 124–125

R

radio buttons, 195

railroad example, 6–7

RAM, 9

range (numeric variables), 27–28

rasterized (bitmapped) image, 133, 137

real numbers, 25, 27

records, 127, 131

recursion, 90, 115–116, 118–119

recursive functions, 115

reentrant functions, 90

registers, 173–174

reports, sorting, 121

requirements (program), defining, 146

resolution (numeric variables), 27–28

rolling dice example, 141–143

runtime error checking, 180

S

scanning, 109–110, 112–113

scope of variables, 67

scoping, 67–68, 70–71

scoping rules, 67

screen objects, designing, 194–195

scripting languages, 187

scroll bars, 195

searching, 109, 112–113

 binary, 116, 118–119

 for records, 131

 using search trees, 101–103

seek function, 128

select statement, 63

senators example, 70–71

separators, statement, 53, 181

servers, 205, 211

sign bit, 28

signed numeric variables, 27

simulations, 141–143

SmallTalk, 157

software, 5–9

software components, 204–205

software development process, 159–160, 162–167

Sorcerer's Apprentice, The, 166

sorting, 121–125

source code modules, 164

source file, 164

spaghetti code, 184

spreadsheet applications, 95, 186

stack pointer, 174

stacks, 89–91

statements, 51, 53–54, 56–57

 grouping, 59

 and program flow, 63–65

statement separators, 53, 181

static control, 195

static variables, 67

status bar, 197

storage, 51, 95

strings

 converting, 35, 181

 determining length of, 35

 representing numbers as, 34

string variables in BASIC, 183

structured programming, 153

structures, 75, 83–84, 86–87, 107

   arrays of, 83

   building, 86–87

   in C++, 202

   linking, 96, 98–99

   naming, 84

subroutines, 51, 59

subtraction, 57

switches, 8, 28

switch statement, 63

symbol table, 150

syntax, 51

T

tables, sorting, 121

tape drives, 8

telecommunications applications, 187

temporary variables, 67

testing (program), 160, 166–167

text boxes, 195

text (or edit) control, 195

text files, 127

text module, 165

text size and color, 196

text variables, 24, 31–35

32-bit processor, 173

ticket queue example, 92–93

toolbar buttons, 196

toolbars, 196–197

top-down program design, 163

transistor switches, 8

translators, 151

transportability, 179

trees, binary search, 101–103

TRUE Boolean value, 37, 39

truth tables, Boolean, 37–39

Turtle Graphics, 12–13

two-dimensional arrays, 78

U

Unicode, 31, 35

uninitialized pointers, 180

United Nations example, 150–151

UNIX, 179

unsigned numeric variables, 27

uppercase, converting, 181, 184–185

user-defined variables, 25, 83

user interface design, 193–197

V

variable address, 21–25

variable-length records, 131

variable names, 22–23

variables, 17–43

   accessing indirectly, 46–47

   array, 77

   assigning, 53, 56

   Boolean, 37–43

   counter, 63

currency, 24

declaring, 21, 67–68, 70–71

dimensioning, 67

lifetime of, 70

managing, 51

mask, 43

numeric, 27–29

public and private, 202

real numbers as, 25

scope of, 67

specialized, 24–25

on the stack, 90

string variables in BASIC, 183

temporary, 67

text, 24, 31–35

types of, 21, 24–25, 29

user-defined, 25, 83

variable types, table of, 29

VB Script, 207

VCR, programming, 213–215

virtual keyword (C++), 203

virtual machine, 15

virtual reality, 141

visibility, 70

Visual Basic, 183

visual programming, 193–197

W

washing-machine program example, 163

water boiling example, 60–61

web browser, 207, 210–211

web server, 210–211

word processors, 187

world–wide web, 207, 210–211

wrapping pointers, 92

X

XOR operation, 37, 39, 57

Z

zero-based array, 109–11